SOCRATES' CRITERIA

A Libertarian Interpretation

Tommi Juhani Hanhijärvi

University Press of America,® Inc.
Lanham · Boulder · New York · Toronto · Plymouth, UK

Copyright © 2012 by
University Press of America,® Inc.
4501 Forbes Boulevard
Suite 200
Lanham, Maryland 20706
UPA Acquisitions Department (301) 459-3366

Estover Road
Plymouth PL6 7PY
United Kingdom

All rights reserved

British Library Cataloging in Publication Information Available

Library of Congress Control Number: 2011938973
ISBN: 978-0-7618-5747-1 (paperback : alk. paper)
eISBN: 978-0-7618-5748-8

To Iso (1918-2010)

If you have form'd a circle to go into,
Go into it yourself, and see how you would do.

Blake ("To God")

CONTENTS:

Preface	ix
Introduction	xiii
1. Good in the *Protagoras*	1
2. Good in the *Hippias Major*	15
3. Good in the *Lysis*	30
4. Right in the *Euthyphro*	50
5. Right in the *Charmides*	55
6. Right in the *Apology*	61
7. Socrates and the *Phaedo*	74
8. Socrates and the *Theaetetus*	82
Conclusion	88
Bibliography	89

PREFACE

This is a very slightly modified version of my doctoral thesis at the Humboldt Universität zu Berlin. Many years have passed since I wrote the thesis. If I had the chance now to make larger changes in this text then I would expand it in scope and length, for I have since found that there is more evidence for the same claims and that their implications are richer. I have not found reasons to take anything back.

However, there have been criticisms, and I would like to take this opportunity to reply to one of them. It is that the terms "free," "good," and "right," or any Greek equivalents to them, do not appear in Socrates, so Socrates cannot be said to have views *about* freedom, good, or right. My critic says I should have spoken instead of such things as virtue or excellence, crafts or skills, fineness or beauty, etc., for these have equivalents in Socrates' Greek: *arête, techne, kalon*.

In reply, to say that such a thing as virtue or fineness is Socrates' topic would have made that topic seem more parochial than it is according to my argument. Virtue, for example, is now a topic among some ethicians and epistemologists, but not at all among all, and also not among various other groups of philosophers or non-philosophers. But freedom is an at least nearly universal concern. Beauty counts in some places, but good and right (as I define them in the Introduction) are properties even of sweet strawberries (which taste good, and may have value intrinsically) and fitting car parts (as the parts are right for their places, or valuable in context)—i.e., in all sorts of places, inevitably. Even current equivalents of Thrasymachus or Callicles care about freedom, good, and right, though they may be as indifferent about beauty as about holiness or kindness. Why is that? *Rational agents* cannot but have purposes, evaluate things, value autonomy, or give reasons, at least to themselves. In my view Socrates means to speak about these things.

What this is to resist most of all is the idea that Socrates is to be understood in some kind of a special context. Someone might say that he is concerned with things uniquely Greek. He may also have a "style" of doing or saying things that needs to be paid attention to. Tacit references to Homer may abound in his utterances. If Socrates were like this then he would not be about arguments—and I think he is all about arguments.

But if Socrates is so cosmopolitan then why does he use locally Greek terms like "arête"? He is Greek, and he speaks with Greeks. Ordinary words are all he has (except for the odd *idea* or *eidos*). He must begin with them.

But notice that this does not mean that he must say only ordinary things. In the early Platonic dialogues something can be *arête* though it is nothing like in Homer even if "arête" is predominantly used as in Homer among Greeks then. Similarly, someone says that rhetoric is a skill, but Socrates says that is not that even remotely. Hippias attributes fineness to gold but Socrates says the fine is self-predicated and gold is clearly not self-predicated. These are radical differences. So Socrates' is not a Protagorean (or Humpty Dumpty) world in which everyone is correct about the objects *they* mean. Rather, in it people use words for things and are *wrong* about them, often.

How then is it possible for Socrates to provide non-ordinary meanings for words like "arête" or "techne"? In general, meaning change is perhaps easiest to picture on an empirical basis, as when a biologist discovers something about tigers or an astronomer about Venus. But Socrates' source of meaning is not empirical: it is structural. He gives examples in everyday language and indicates relations between these. (A quite elementary relation would be analogy: as the mouse stands to the piece of cheese, so the cat stands to the mouse.) Socrates' message consists of such relations. More exactly, whatever has these relations is free—or, good, right, excellent, skilful, fine, etc.

However, Socrates does not himself invent special words for the relations (except for the occasional *idea* or *eidos*) and this is the reason why one's choice of terms can *never* match Socrates'. I.e, his are not there to be matched. E.g. "kalon" is not a descriptive word for any of them. Nor, for that matter, are "free," "good," or "right." These single words should not be clung to. I could have used others of my own in the place, e.g. "autonomy," "intrinsic value," and "duty," but these too would have been imperfect. And if Socrates had been a Finn he would have used different words again (believe me). But he could have presented exactly the same relations. Socrates' wavelength is this long, so to speak. His meanings are not in single words, or in sentences, but further out there. One needs many many words, and many sentences, before the appropriate variations are exposed.

But is it then not misleading of Socrates not to use technical words in the place of "arête" and other ordinary ones? Should he not have marked his wavelength somehow? Personally I feel that Socrates would have benefited from introducing *more* special symbols. There could have been a practical philosopher's *plus* and *minus*, for example, or an elemantary map of grammatical moods, presented at the later stages of each of his dialogues. This might have helped his interpreters across the ages to see that his message is formal. Even then his interpreters would have always needed to study his examples and the relations that obtain between them, for otherwise they could not have understood his code. So even then any *translations of his words* would have been completely beside the point. But at least it would have been more obvious that there is a code to crack at all.

But the cost of using only or too many technical words, or too early in each new social contact, is clearly also there. That cost is isolation and irrelevance. For technical enough contexts can seem self-sufficient, lacking entirely in external uses. Ultimately there could be a symbolism purely about certain symbols, vacuously. Using a word like "arête" in ancient Greece is a means to break out of such a circle and to have relevance in a life common to all. (Using "virtue" today is *not* such a means.) One needs to begin from what people care about and use their words. And then, because speakers have the capacity to abstract, one can break away from traditional associations.

I am aware that this sort of a universalistic position is unpopular today. Many kinds of universalists are now accused of being biased. But notice that such a culture of debunking may itself be biased. Perhaps we are today quietistic in avoiding confrontations. A universalistic Socrates was more popular many times before. He is assigned a permanent importance by the anti-totalitarians Karl Popper and Hannah Arendt writing after World War II. The existentialists Kierkegaard and Nietzsche nearly worship him, placing him right next to Jesus and sometimes above, while their own century is keener on regional and historical variations. The Renaissance intellectual Erasmus admires him seemingly as a humanist and not as a figure fitted only to a single age. And of course there is Plato himself, making perhaps the boldest claims possible. I would not confidently predict that we will see a comeback of great, universalizing intellectuals like this in the near future. But at least it is a pity if we rule out possible lessons from history *a priori*, by insisting that there cannot be any before we even study the sources.

I hope I have now answered my critic.

Now to thanks. I wish to thank all of my philosophical friends in Heidelberg, Berlin, Amsterdam, and Helsinki for the sympathetic conversations over the years. There were countless hours spent at libraries, parks, cafes, and street corners, and philosophy was not separate from theater, music, or parties. Even a museum could stimulate speculation or debate. Some of it was quite personal and emotional. This was a very large classroom. I consider myself very fortunate to have been allowed into it.

I dedicate this book to my grandfather, in memory of his long and admirable life.

Helsinki, December 6th 2010   TJH

INTRODUCTION

My aim in this book is to interpret some of the views expressed by the figure of "Socrates" in what are currently often thought to be Plato's earlier dialogues.[1]

This Introduction is devoted to some of the general properties of this discussion (i-x). The actual discussion is easier to understand if they are observed first. I will not address most of them again in later chapters (1-8).

(i) My *thesis* is that Socrates is a "libertarian." By this I mean that in his characteristic quest for definitions he is for freedom.[2] In accordance with this, his audience consists of agents who contemplate plans of action and not of e.g. scientists or analysts who seek to explain or understand things. What he seeks to give such agents are tools for their own independent thought. It is in this sense that he is a libertarian: he liberates, or gives what is needed for freedom.

The idea is not that definitions relate to freedom only instrumentally. Rather, defining or seeking definitions *is* freedom. Socrates wants agents to think for themselves, as an end in itself. This thinking is in language and not for instance pictures, so in practice Socrates attempts to get agents to speak for themselves. This speech, in turn, is in principle public, so one cannot use Socrates' tools and then as an effect of this be free in private thought or feeling. This is how things would be if each of us had her own and special way of thinking or being free. Things are not like that for Socrates. Instead, there is one size to fit all. For freedom consists of the use of his tools. Due to this, one can check whether someone is free, for she either speaks in a certain way or she does not—that is all. If she does not then one can explain to her why she should, and how she could. This, too, would be a linguistic and public process. So if someone is liberated then she does not need to observe anything, as e.g. the behaviour of Spartans or the orbits of the stars. No special feeling is necessary. And she also does not need to have certain additional properties, like maturity in age, either gender, etc. Talking does it all.

There are several ways in which this could be wrong. Many have said that the free do not necessarily act at all but that they are only *able* to if they want to, and that they may not want to, perhaps ever. If they are correct then Socrates is on the wrong track completely. Also, if to be free is to take any kind of *un*thinking action, or to perceive or introspect something one has trouble expressing, then Socrates would definitely not be correct in teaching his interlocutors as he does. Their self-interest would then not require that they pay attention to his characteristic questions or demands. As self-interested agents they could safely ignore him. His rules about definitions, his puzzles or paradoxes, and his intrusive impatience would then all be only an irrelevant nuisance to the free. If, in turn, he is correct about freedom that it is public in his sense then not only his interlocutors but also many recent philosophical and less reflected views about it are misled. For it is far from customary among either group now to picture freedom in the way that he does. So if I am correct about Socrates—that he is correct about freedom—then major changes are called for in contemporary thought, and not only about Socrates. And in that case he is no ancient relic but of great relevance today and tomorrow.

A further possibility is that *Socrates* is not a libertarian of this sort. It could be that when he does what is so characteristic of him—seeks definitions—he is after something other than freedom. He may want to explain certain meanings, give causal accounts, engage in epistemology in general, or something else. That his search for definitions has to do with freedom is a novel view in the current literature, as (ix) below will illustrate.

(ii) This book's is not a total account of Socrates' views. For I will consider only *selected* passages and dialogues from Plato's earlier phase. In other words, the interpretive (historical) scope of my discussion is quite limited. I do not think that I need to explain why my scope is not narrower, but why is it not broader? For three reasons (a-c).

(a) The passages in question seem to justify the attribution of features to the early Platonic Socrates that are *peculiar* to him. If one wants to study the Socrates of Plato's early dialogues in particular, then one should focus on these passages and features. He does have further features but they can be studied without invoking him. His views about military valor, for example, are not unique. One can study the same views in others. The following of Socrates' views seem to be peculiar to him. He seeks to refute others and to be refuted by them in plain, non-technical language; he views "virtue" as consisting of either ethical knowledge or inquiry; and he attributes intrinsic value to all and only "self-predicated" things.

I note in chapters 7 and 8 that the middle and later Plato departs from all three views to some extent. In general, other philosophers are still further away from him (which is a thesis impossible to expand on here).

(b) The passages in question appear to express what Socrates is *most concerned* to communicate. (It is only an accident that what he wants most to say is also peculiar to him as in (a).) Hence to study them in particular seems to be charitable, for then one takes Socrates at his word, trusting his powers of judgement as to what is serious and what is not.

The less serious things he says are not easy to classify. He uses irony; there are loose analogies between things that happen to be familiar to his interlocutors; and there are hypotheses that turn out to fail when scrutinized (by Socrates or an interlocutor).

How do the seriously intended elements stand out from the rest? They are never successfully questioned by Socrates or his interlocutors. Second, they solve problems that are presented as rationally compelling, such as the well-known paradox of inquiry and what I will call the "paradox of the will."

This is not to say that the less serious parts or aspects deserve in general to be ignored or skipped by readers. They are not simply useless entertainment or blunders. For one can think of them as context-relative preliminaries. It is e.g. only self-important interlocutors (and readers) that need ironic treatment, and to different interlocutors different analogies will be familiar and different hypotheses relevant. After such context-sensitive preliminaries Socrates can finally come to the serious content which is remarkably stable throughout the earlier Platonic dialogues. But it will not be a part of my argument to indicate why several passages do *not* seem to qualify as serious. For seriousness is a requirement for attention in this essay.

(c) Socrates *himself* practices and preaches selectivity. Hence, if one said that all of his views are correct then one would in a sense contradict him, paradoxical as this may sound. If one wants to be charitable towards him then one must be selective. On Socrates' norms, if a poet is quoted then only briefly. The quotation is interpreted as meaningful per se, not as receiving meaning only once it is taken in the cultural context of the poet (whatever that would be). So it is abstracted from its original context. If one does not advocate or practice this norm then one cannot call oneself a friendly interpreter of Socrates in a full sense.[3]

I hope it is understandable by now why this book is selective in its approach and not holistic. It is in fact so selective that it will not be a survey of *any* dialogue's total content. Every early Platonic dialogue consists of a wealth of ideas and my task is not to give any overview of them. Many other works seek to do this.

(iii) I will quote Plato only very rarely and briefly, and more broadly I will leave philological issues to others.

Again I have a few reasons for adopting my policy. First, others are more capable at philological issues that I am, for my Greek is weak. Second, Socrates seems like an excellent example for when philological nuances matter comparatively little. For he defines his key terms through analogies. Given that he uses many different analogies, no single one needs to be perfect and none the less his meaning can be specific. The wanted meanings are established in this process. Due to this, his Greek is not ordinary in the vital passages. He creates a theoretic vocabulary to suit his purposes, and everyday language (as he finds it before his theorizing, that is) does not contain that vocabulary. (It may none the less contain the same *words*, but with largely different meanings. An example is *arête*. *Idea* and *eidos* are to my knowledge examples of terms that had no everyday use in Socrates' surroundings.) He does, of course, explain his new meanings by invoking old meanings (given that he does not use ostension), so the old meanings do need to be interpreted even if Socrates' new meanings are different from them. Otherwise the new meanings could not be understood. But those old meanings are always intended as entirely trivial and explicit. They are not nuanced. They do not, hence, seem to demand special philological attention.

(iv) I will use several illustrative *examples* of my own design. Their purpose is to make Socrates' patterns more understandable. It should be observed that their purpose is not to attribute to him a substantial ethical position to which he does not explicitly adhere. Socrates himself provides rather few examples of intrinsically valuable things in particular. Yet it seems to be in his spirit to use examples and not e.g. formalizations, and this is why I resort to examples of my own.

(v) My *terminology* will not be Socrates' own. My terms are not even translations of his. For example, I will not use "virtue" or "excellence" for *arête*, but "right."

These are the terms I will use repeatedly in interpreting Socrates' views: "criterion," "good," "right," and "will." Here is how:

- *Criterion*. Nearly every question which Socrates poses seriously expresses, and requires the satisfaction of, a "criterion." A criterion says what is necessary and sufficient of its object (i.e., whatever it is a criterion for). In a specifically epistemological use, a criterion for x renders x recognizable (identifiable). It guides one to x. The thought is that x may not be easy to recognize without the criterion but that recognition comes easily with its help. It must also be noticed, however, that a perfect criterion may actually fail in practice, for it may be difficult to *find* what meets a criterion C though for any possible x one sees exactly how to decide whether x meets C or not—what *would* meet C *if* it came along. In general, a criterion provides decisive news about its object.

Using the word "criterion" in crucial places is not quite the same as using "definition" or "account" in them because "criterion" is more obviously normative or epistemological. This is to abide by my general argument on which Socrates' interest is not explanatory but normative. But I will use these other terms also, as well as "standard," "measure," and "test," when the choice of words is not so critical.[4]

- *Good* and *right*. The criteria come in two sets, one set for "good" and the other for "right." Being good is being intrinsically valuable, i.e. valuable in abstraction from other things. Being right is being a means to good and an extrinsic end. An extrinsic end is something valuable as an end but only when accompanied by something that is not.[5]

The reason to adopt these terms instead of Socrates' own is that, as was noted in (iii), Socrates seeks to redirect our attention. Where we have approved certain things before, we should with him begin to approve others in their stead. Given this, the use of terms with more or less firm descriptive contents like "virtue" would lead us to ignore the Socratic message. We would then be prepared to hear something Aristotelian and less intellectual or something Christian and self-sacrificial and Socrates' more radical position would pass us by. We would be tied to the descriptive contents that the word has already. We are not tied down in that way if we use normative place holders like he does. "Good" and "right" are such normative place holders for us. For we can use "good" for a strawberry, a car, and so on. There are no limits to the application of words like this one and this is why the use of such words is possible to reform.

- *Will.* Some of the criteria refer to "the will" or to willing. This is here a very general term which does not exclude desires or preferences of any kind. I will use "want," "desire," and "prefer" as synonyms for "will."

I should warn the reader that even though I speak of the will in the context of Socrates I do not mean that he is modern in the sense of thinking of such a "faculty" (in the sense of Kant, for example). The meaning of this term is much looser than that in this book. It has no rational or moral implications. One can "will" anything under the sky.

Here are some further uses that may differ from the reader's: I use "ethical" for first-order value in general (e.g., what ought to exist for its own sake, whether as accompanied by another thing or not) and "moral" for the value of serving another agent's interest (but not necessarily to the exclusion of one's own). "Normative" encompasses first- and second-order (epistemic) value. "Epistemic" properties make things recognizable for what they are and "metaphysical" ones apply to them descriptively. "Analytic" relations cannot be consistently denied (Kant) or sensibly questioned (Moore).[6]

The nature of criteria, good, normativity, etc., will be at issue much of the time below, so they will all be conceived more strongly than above. I want to show that it is Socrates who views them in those stronger ways, so I want to keep my framework thin until Socrates' views are mapped on to it. If I did not keep the framework thin, then it would not be interpretive findings that justified its adoption for it would be accepted dogmatically in advance of study. That I have a framework of terms and concepts in advance at all does not by itself make me a dogmatist, however, because I will claim to show in what ways Socrates' themes and assertions accord with my framework.[7]

(vi) I will not go into the so-called "Socratic problem" whether Plato's Socrates is the historically real Socrates in any dialogue or passage, for I have nothing to contribute to this debate. My interest in this essay is in what the early Plato wants to say whether or not the historical Socrates said those things.

(vii) The motivation for this discussion is easier to understand if it is noted what *problems* are easily felt to apply to Socrates by current readers.

A first problem arises because Socrates creates his own demand. Nobody longs for the arrival of a Socrates before he arrives. Rather, he comes along and then he finds reasons why he with his particular traits and abilities should be thought useful for anything. The situation is different for, say, a medical doctor, because physical diseases exist, are recognized as evils, and are thought of as curable by medical doctors. Metaphorically speaking, Socrates begins by spreading a disease that he can cure. Everyday thinking is not explicit that such a disease exists at all or needs curing. Hence one asks what entitles Socrates to spread the disease in the first place. Why does he not just stand back and let Athenians pursue what they do, living and letting live? Why not let them keep their religions, for example, no matter how irrational they are? Who needs a philosopher?

The second problem is that Socrates attempts to cure by requiring *definitions*. This is strange. A definition or the act of giving one does not look like a cure of any kind. How should it help anyone? So why does Socrates require definitions? Are not valuable things very different from defined objects and from acts of defining something? If they are, how can definitions be helpful? Why are they necessary? Also, Socrates seems to "self-predicate" good by requiring the particular *sorts* of definitions that he does, and hence he can seem to confuse predication with identity and universals with particulars.[8] Moreover, he may appear to *base* on the same everyday intuitions (by collecting them into definitions) that he wants to revise, which would be circular. So not only does it seem misplaced to require definitions: the definitions he requires seem additionally to be confused. These are ways to suspect that Socrates' type of philosophizing is irrational.

Both of these problems, the social and the logical, have a contemporary ring. They are motivated especially by values and theories that have emerged long after Socrates' time. The first problem arises particularly for liberals who stress the value of tolerance in society. Socrates is not a liberal like this. He is for public criticism, not tolerance. (This is not to say that he is intolerant if someone wears unconventional clothes, or speaks with a foreign accent, etc. He is not *in*tolerant.) The second problem arises with a new urgency due to recent doubts about the role of definitions in philosophy. The later Wittgenstein doubts their need. Logicians like Russell see their need but view Socrates (or Plato) as eminently confused about them.

These problems regarding Socrates are solvable by viewing him as a libertarian. For he says that the free need definite aims, and it is because of this that the free need definitions. This is why Socrates or any philosopher like him has a role in public life. Freedom requires criticism. Moreover, his techniques are more exotic than recent philosophers have tended to think so he is not guilty of their fallacies.

It is essential to notice how the social and logical problems do not really appear to be separate in Socrates' mind. For he seems to say that it is *authority* in general that requires definitions. Authority must be publicly accountable. A public account, however, is at its best a definition. A definition makes its content explicit briefly and clearly, and perhaps at best with self-evidence. The alternative to definitions is secrecy. There could be a secret society that has control in a country, or one could habitually obey something that one does not explicitly agree to or affect. In both cases the lack of freedom would be due to the same thing from a Socratic point of view.

(viii) This book will proceed in the following order. First come three chapters (1-3) about good, then three chapters about right (4-6). Then follow two chapters about the middle and later Plato (7-8) and finally there is a short conclusion. Here are the approximate contents of the chapters:

- 1 (*Protagoras*): Socrates says that if x is good then *only* x is good. He means by this, first, that good is the same in many different contexts, so those contexts do not involve different senses of good. So there cannot be two goods. This is not to say that two different objects cannot be good, but that that by virtue of which they are good must be the same in both cases. Secondly, he intends that good is "primitive." (x is primitive iff there is a possible world which contains x but no non-x. Some call properties like this "lonely.") Exclusiveness can be said to imply primitiveness but not conversely.

Why would one agree to predicate good only of what is exclusive in the above sense? Does one abuse words if one does not do so? Is this what Socrates says? No. Rather, one needs to distinguish x clearly from non-x so that one can view it transparently. Then one is aware of x. This is a condition of free decision, for one cannot choose what one is not aware of. For example, Hippocrates cannot consciously seek to be educated by a sophist if he has no clear conception of a sophist. He is leaping into the dark in preferring what he does. But if he wants to make voluntary choices then he needs distinct objects, for to choose what one cannot see is not to choose it voluntarily. It is rather to sacrifice one's deliberative role.

This is to argue that one's self-interest ultimately requires an exclusive view of good. So a practical problem faces one if one does not satisfy Socrates' criterion: one's own freedom is confined.

There are problems with the *Protagoras'* view, however. First, requiring exclusiveness may be fine as it is but it is not informative. It is to speak of a vague utopia and not to advise how to get there. It is as if one replied to the question, "What is x?" with: "x is something quite different from other things." That would not be much of an answer. Second, being primitive just does not seem to be the same as being good. Nor is good recognizable by its being one or primitive, for properties other than good seem to be primitive (e.g. perhaps yellow). So whether or not this criterion is necessary it seems insufficient. Third, from an evaluative perspective it can seem unnecessary also, for the activity of individuation may be distinct from or even hostile to any activity of evaluation. For evaluation can seem like a very different activity from the summing and dividing often associated with logical individuation.

Due to these problems the *Protagoras'* view appears incorrect. None the less it is not utterly misled, as further chapters explain.

• 2 (*Hippias Major*): In this dialogue Socrates "self-predicates" good. A good thing is at once a standard for good things in general and the best instance on that standard. I will reject an analytical interpretation of self-predication and defend an evaluative and pragmatic one. On this view, good is not simply a primitive universal (as it was in chapter 1) but an evaluative relation. This is to be directed at itself. So a good thing evaluates itself, and if it does so successfully then it affirms itself, and only itself in particular. In so doing it provides evidence for its own value and individuates itself. This kind of an object is also possible to construe as pragmatically consistent, i.e. as practicing what it preaches, if its content is appropriate.

The rational benefit of viewing ends in this manner is that now ends are not distinct from reasons to prefer them. They do not need external contextualization. They do not need to be viewed in a certain light as opposed to another, for they provide their own interpretations and contexts. Therefore the objections raised to the *Protagoras'* position in chapter 1 now appear to be avoidable.

But the *Hippias Major* does not explain how a self-satisfied thing can be for itself in the sense of wanting anything at all, for after all it already has all that it wants. Socrates presents this problem (which I will call the "paradox of the will") in the *Lysis* and responds to it in the same dialogue.

- 3 (*Lysis*): In this dialogue, good is regularly predicated of desires. That is, it is good to will something or other, and in one way or another. Second, in this dialogue good things are causally effective in producing things distinct from themselves, namely the ends which they are for. So causally self-sufficient desires are good.

This avoids the "paradox of the will" only if not only the effects but also the causes of the relevant chains have intrinsic value. So we need to think of causal chains of ends, and more exactly of evolving evaluative processes, as good. These are not repetitive "loops" like in chapter 2. But they are not entirely free-floating either, for as before the good need to be distinct. They must be patterned. Performative verbs are best used to explain them. Here is the focal point of Socrates' view of good on my interpretation. Now we see why defining is a free activity.

- 4 (*Euthyphro*): In this dialogue Socrates says that right things are identified extrinsically to themselves and on a standard that is multiply and economically applicable. Hence, right is a different type of thing than good. Good is self-relational, right is rather the converse—"other-relational," if you will. But they are similar in that each is a single and specific standard. Right is decisive between all possible candidate cases of right, from without. It is not itself an instance of right. Good in chapters 1-3 was a measure specifically for itself, from within.

But somewhat unfairly to his interlocutors Socrates never tells them outside of the *Apology* why he theorizes right as he does. In this chapter (4), we can wonder especially why Socrates is being this severe about "piety," a bearer of value.

- 5 (*Charmides*): This time Socrates says that right has positive value in all negative contexts. Good does not have this feature. To invoke a favourite analogy of Socrates', medicine (right) is unlike health (good). Medicine has value relationally to evil (disease) but health does not relate positively to evil. Health, conversely, is valuable as divorced from evil but medicine is not. But right is also unlike medicine, for its value is relational to *all* evils. Also, Socratic good was of course already described as quite unlike medically ensured health.

Like the criterion in chapter 4, this one in chapter 5 is left somewhat in the air by Socrates. He does not seem to explain his motive for demanding that there be only a *single* extrinsic value outside the *Apology*. For all we know there might as well be many different ones or none at all. Second, the relation between the criteria in 4 and 5 is not explained more than allusively outside the *Apology*.

- 6 (*Apology*): In this dialogue Socrates says that right is social inquiry into good. Right action is effective against the things he views as evil, e.g. boastfulness, aimlessness, inactivity. It is not merely valuable alongside such evils (as it was in chapter 5), for it actually converts them from their negativity. But right things are effective in this way precisely because right things need to be judged from without (and this fits with the criterion in chapter 4). Hence, what Socrates says about right in the *Apology* implies what he says about it in the *Euthyphro* and the *Charmides* as these were presented in chapters 4 and 5.

In this dialogue Socrates also exposes his motive for speaking of right as he does. For by the criteria in 2 and 3 it is exactly the good who can identify good. The non-good, consequently, cannot do this. But they ought to become good (or they face the problems described in chapters 1 and 2). How then are they to seek this end? Their only apparently possible response is to cross-question everyone indiscriminately, and this step Socrates takes early in his career (as he tells us in the *Apology*). Rich and poor, young and old qualify as prospective teachers. All the non-good know is, ultimately, that they need help from without. Because they cannot discriminate between authoritative and non-authoritative informants in advance of hearing their thoughts, they need to welcome lessons from all.

In this chapter (6) I also argue that those acting right are moral in the sense that they favour others' free thought and expression. But given that it is in one's self-interest to become good and one attains this aim only by doing right, there is now a sense in which it is in one's self-interest to be moral.

- 7 and 8 (*Phaedo, Theaetetus*): In these chapters I compare the middle and later Plato's Socrates' (henceforth: SOCRATES') views in the *Phaedo* and the *Theaetetus* to those presented in chapters 1-6 (i.e., Socrates'). A first generalization will be that there is little change on the essentials. Ends are self-predicated and social inquiry into them is the generally applicable means to them. A second generalization is that in so far as the SOCRATES of the *Phaedo* contradicts the early Socrates he contradicts the *Theaetetus*' SOCRATES also, and conversely. So these later-than-early dialogues do not exhibit any single consistent alternative to the early Socrates.[9] This indicates that the author who described (and presumably understood) the earlier views does not later find fault in them, at least not any fault he could correct.

I conclude that it is warranted to view Socrates as a libertarian.

(ix) *Others' interpretations* of the early Plato's Socrates are too many and varied to be surveyed briefly. I will now compare two recent interpretations with mine, Terry Penner's and Terence Irwin's.

In "The Unity Of Virtue" Penner denies that Socrates is after "meanings" of ordinary ethical concepts (though this is not the only thesis he defends in this article). For instance courage might turn out not to share properties with an ordinary stereotype of it. For Socrates contradicts ordinary intuitions, saying e.g. that there is only one virtue. This would not be possible if he based on everyday intuitions. Thus far Penner's position accords with mine.[10]

Penner is rather unhelpful on the positive side, however. Instead of a meaning, Socrates wants a "referent," he says, and more particularly a universal that is the efficient cause of the notion he inquires into (i.e. X in Socrates' typical "What is X?"). The cause may share no properties with the effect (X). But how is the cause identified? Penner does not address this issue, though the identification of causes is in general problematic in many ways (see Psillos and Sosa, ed.). Hence, to tell us that Socrates is after causes not meanings is not to tell us much about what he wants to be done.

But I also claim to detect in Penner an outright fault. For him, Socrates accepts everyday examples of virtues. He is dissatisfied merely with ordinary views of the causes of these exemplary things. So he is not a reformist in ethics. He seeks instead either to explain values by their causes or to provide information about means for preconceived ends (or both). But apparently Socrates does want to revise ends. This is most obvious in the *Apology*. Athens has fallen asleep and seeks wealth and honour where it should seek some sort of normative self-knowledge. This is one among many passages that I will cite as indicating that Socrates wants to change values. Hence, though Penner seems correct to deny the central role of analysis in Socrates, what he advocates instead does not seem Socratic.

Irwin says that Socrates requires definitions in ethics so that disputes in that field can be resolved. Outside ethics we get along acceptably without definitions, and it is a special feature of ethics that its subject matter is disputed. It is not a field in which publicly accepted conclusions are reached. Definitions, however, can provide us with standards. Socrates asks for definitions so that certain normative problems become solvable, Irwin says.

If Irwin is correct then Socrates needs to contradict at least some everyday evaluative intuitions. It would not do to simply report disagreements to solve them. One must make some independent move or the contradictions will remain. How can Socrates do this? What is the independent authority he invokes? Irwin says he uses a "craft analogy." The crafts have certain things in common due to which they can solve problems or disputes. They are teachable and commonly accepted authorities. The thought is that if ethics can be transformed into a craft, or into something that resembles one, then ethics will begin to solve disputes just like the (other) crafts already do.

Apparently the only correct aspect of this is the epistemological motive. But even it does not quite fit Socrates. For Socrates does not begin by finding Athenians in conflict about values. Rather, in his view there is too *little* conflict. Indeed he induces conflict. He is a "gadfly." Socrates himself drives his interlocutors into contradictions. Athens is asleep, not too restless. So even though Socrates is after standards in ethics, he seems not to be mainly after consistency. He values certain other things more than consistency per se. I will argue that these include free decision, open inquiry, self-evidence, and self-sufficiency. He does value consistency also, but not for its own sake. One is to be consistent with the aforementioned values, not consistent simpliciter. These values Irwin seems not to explore, however. So he seems to ignore Socrates' actual criteria.

Also the craft analogy (not only the demand of consistency per se) seems to have much less importance than Irwin believes. It is indisputable that Socrates relies on analogies with the various crafts to express his ideas. But this leaves open the issue how much these analogies are intended to convey about what he is really after. They are not the only analogies he draws, as everyone knows. They are also contested (see e.g. *Charmides* 166B-C, 168A, *Republic* 1 337A-C, 335C-D[11]). When the craft analogy is objected to, the objection is not that the crafts lack authority or that Socrates is wrong about them but rather that they do not resemble ethics in the relevant respects. Because the analogy fails to hold at important points, Socrates cannot use the analogy to justify his criteria. Sometimes the analogies hold and sometimes they do not, just like so many others that Socrates draws. More dramatically, none of the problems or criteria which Socrates aims at expressing are found in any single craft he cites (let alone all of them). For example, none of the crafts he cites features definitions, but undeniably Socrates views definitions as indicating ethical authority. His demands (questions) are not *from* the crafts. The craft analogy is useful on some points but not on others, so Irwin exaggerates its importance.[12]

(x) I will be offering *objections* to Socrates to measure his ideas from an independent standpoint. These are mainly inspired by Aristotle, Hume, Nietzsche, and the later Wittgenstein and their recent followers. I will work with what I take to be simplified versions of their views. I will not refer to their originators, for to ensure that I understand them correctly would result in too many complications and detours.

The objections I consider are far from being the only possible ones. The ones I consider receive particularly informative replies based on Socrates, and that is why I have chosen them.

Notes

1. The ones at issue will be, most prominently and in the order of their appearance in this text, the *Protagoras*, the *Hippias Major*, the *Lysis*, the *Euthyphro*, the *Charmides*, and the *Apology*, but also, in lesser roles, the *Gorgias*, *Republic* 1, the *Ion*, the *Cratylus*, the *Hippias Minor*, and the *Laches*. In chapters 7 and 8 I will briefly go into the *Phaedo* and the *Theaetetus*. The *Phaedo* is probably a middle-period dialogue and the *Theaetetus* a later one. For currently widely held views about the chronological order of Plato's dialogues, see Fine, "Introduction," p. 1n1, and Penner, "Socrates And The Early Dialogues."

2. A "libertarian" is, as I believe everyone will agree, defined as an advocate of liberty (freedom). This is what Socrates is according to my argument. I do *not* mean that he *opposes causal determinism* like many current 'libertarians' in metaphysics do. For unlike them he theorizes and propagates freedom *intrinsically* and not comparatively to something else (such as causal determinism).

The intrinsic identification of freedom does not now mean only that the free are ultimately identified non-comparatively. It means also that they are identified by themselves, as self-determining agents. This makes the view of freedom in the early Platonic dialogues especially strong. Current views in general require far less of the free; see Watson on them.

"Libertarian" also has social or political uses on which a libertarian is for laissez-faire capitalism (like Nozick) or socialist anarchism (like Chomsky). Socrates' views are too abstract to have such social or political implications directly. He is rather for the freedom of thought or speech than for any particular type of economy, concrete judicial system, etc. His is not a system of criminal justice or an economy of goods. Clearly his libertarianism presupposes the absence of material need and violent danger, but he appears to have no serious views as to how such needs and dangers are best eliminated.

3. But actually Socrates goes further than this and here I do not wish to follow him. For his norm is that if x quotes y (a poet, e.g.) then x must defend the quote in question. x is responsible for saying why the quote deserves attention. x brought it up in the first place, and y is not present. (This is not to be taken as a denial of the possibility of self-evidence. In chapters 2 and 3 Socrates will defend self-evidence, but it is acts—not artefacts like poems—that are self-evident.) If I treated Socrates in this way, I could not say that he is plausible due to things *he* says; the defences would be mine; but I do not wish to do this because I believe the defences I will present in fact to be his.

4. Fregean "senses" might also have been made use of, but this would have required some prior—and controversial—clarification about what they *are*.

5. This is to tie down the use of these words somewhat, for not everyone uses these words specifically for intrinsic and extrinsic value. For example, some apply "good" also to extrinsically valuable things. But I would stress that the change is not great. Moreover, philosophers have tended to use "good" and "right" like this, at least in the past century. Thus compare Moore and Ross. "Good" things have value intrinsically. What is "right" is normally something instrumental to good (as in utilitarianism) *or* something to which one has a duty no matter what its effects (think of Kant's categorical imperative, or Ross' prima facie duties). In my definition above "right" means both of these things. This definition will turn out to fit with the things that Socrates says in chapters 4-6. In other words, Socrates is not simply a consequentialist *or* a deontologist: he is both.

6. I will rely on analyticity but cannot explore or defend the notion in this book.

7. This framework of terms is, as one might say, weakly libertarian, because if Socrates has standards ("criteria") for intrinsic value ("good") and for means or applied ends ("right") then he has views about rational agency. I doubt that anyone would dispute that he is a weak libertarian. But still it is a further thing to be a libertarian in the strong or philosophical sense of defending the liberty of defining something or of searching for certain kinds of definition. Weak libertarianism does not commit one to strong libertarianism, and my terms are only weakly libertarian though I argue for Socrates' strong libertarianism by using them.

8. Chapter 2 will elaborate on these supposed confusions, but to avoid being cryptic now let me note that Socrates has been said to confuse the "is" of "Superman is fast" with that of "Superman is Clark Kent," as if *fast* in the first sentence picked out someone in

particular and hence read like "Superman is fastest" or implied that fastness is a particular.

Existence, or the "is" of "Superman is x," where x is anything at all and Superman consequently exists, seems to become a major issue only in the middle dialogues.

9. We do not need to survey further dialogues to draw this conclusion. But the hypothesis that *some* of Plato's later-than-early dialogues contain a consistent alternative to Socrates is not hereby contradicted.

10. Earlier in the 20th century it was usual to view Socrates as an analyst of everyday norms and then to be baffled by his errors as such an analyst. A "Socratic fallacy" was viewed as applying to all who prioritize definitions. Penner, by contrast, does not view Socrates as a failed analyst.

11. For instance, *Republic* 334A-B says that a medical doctor is effective not only in curing diseases but also in inflicting them—by virtue of the same power—and 335C-D says that the just can make others only just, not unjust. The causal power is of a different sort in the two cases, not analogical.

12. A third aspect of Irwin's interpretation is *eudaemonism*. Especially in the *Euthydemus* Socrates seems to praise "happiness" as a universal end. It is not easy to understand what this means. Obviously Socrates does not mean that everyone should want merely to feel good, for instance. Does he mean that all should want to "flourish" in some sense? Which sense? In my view, Socrates does not develop ideas along these lines. *Eudaemonia* seems to be for him a contentless and general term of approval, not like anything with a distinct and substantial content. Vlastos' "Happiness And Virtue In Socrates' Moral Theory" (*Socrates*, pp. 200-232) supports this view from a philological perspective. From a systematic viewpoint, some main problems of welfarism are surveyed by Scarre.

Chapter 1

GOOD IN THE *PROTAGORAS*

Socrates consistently maintains that good is a special property. In the *Protagoras*, he gives us some initial leads about how it is that. It is "exclusive," as I will say, being the only thing to apply specifically to all the things in a certain realm, namely to good things. Nothing but this property is to be found in all good things and only in them. I will say that exclusiveness for Socrates implies "primitiveness," so that good is not always accompanied by any specific other thing. For the *only* thing common and specific to all good things should be this property, good. Nothing should ride piggy-back on it and it should not ride piggy-back on anything else. (Alternative terms for "primitive" would be e.g. "independent," "separate," "lonely.") Everything else will shift with good things, only not this property. These points I will present in 1.1.

This same view of good is found also in the *Hippias Major* (1.2.) and the *Lysis* (1.3.). Hence we see that it is not an isolated one for Socrates. He does not express it only now and then but at several serious junctures. In these junctures the identification of intrinsic value is sought. Exclusiveness is required to help us in this search. It is a tool, a technique—a "criterion." (But it is not the criterion itself that is good, of course. It is not a good thing and it is not the property good. The criterion is but a means, a map, to good and good things. Good and good things will relate intimately in chapters 2 and 3 but not yet in this chapter, 1.)

In 1.4.-1.6. I clarify what Socrates means by requiring exclusiveness of good. The point is not that good things are all to be exactly alike to each other but that that by which they can be distinguished from other things needs to be the same in every case (1.4.). The reason to view good as exclusive is practical not descriptive or explanatory (1.5.). For one needs a unique good to deliberate consistently and consciously. It must stand out. E.g., Hippocrates cannot seek instruction from a sophist without having a clear view of what he is after. He must be able to separate a sophist from a non-sophist in advance. If he lacks a distinct aim, he cannot consciously take aim, nor hence will anything properly. (To illustrate, I would not take aim at all if I what I "aimed" at would be described by me as "schrümpf," because I do not know how to tell schrümpf things apart from others (nobody does, as it is not a word). I am not *aware* of schrümpf things, hence. But if I am unaware of something, surely I cannot choose it either, or be for it, will it, etc.) So it is one's freedom that ultimately requires a unique, a distinct good—a Socratic definition. One must find a good of this sort or one is not free. But one wishes to be free: that desire is basic to all whom Socrates addresses. For his audience consists of egoists who contemplate what to do.[1]

In 1.6. I present the objection that requiring exclusiveness or primitiveness of good is not per se entirely fair to practical agents unless the specialness of aims is itself practically measured. For if decisions about what is exclusive or primitive belong to e.g. metaphysicians or scientists (who are not practically interested) then Socrates is requiring free agents to deny their own decisional role, and for the sake of their freedom. This would be paradoxical. In chapters 2 and 3 we will see that this is not Socrates' meaning, for the exclusiveness and primitiveness that he requires is teleological. He wants things individuated by certain normative functions. So in requiring that good be viewed as unique (distinct, precise) Socrates does not mean to confine egoists from without but to enable them from within. For they want those normative functions when they understand what those functions are about. But in this chapter, 1, we will not yet advance that far.

1.1. Exclusive (Hence also Primitive)

In one segment of the *Protagoras*, Socrates begins his interrogation of Protagoras by finding Protagoras' assent to the view that not all lives are as well lived as others (351B). He wants next to pinpoint what distinguishes these types of lives from each other. He proposes that the difference is hedonic, so that to live in a pleased way is to live well (351B-C). But as against this Protagoras sees some painful things as valuable and some pleasing things as negative (351D). However, this does not show that pleasure is not good, Socrates says, for pleasure can be good despite this appearance. For if pleasure is good then it does not matter if it has negative (painful) consequences (353C-354E). Conversely, if pleasure is good then painful things can have value as means to pleasures (ibid.). Then only pleasure would have intrinsic value. Hence, ethical hedonism can be correct even though Protagoras said it was not. For Protagoras ignored the means/ends distinction. If he observes that distinction, Socrates is saying, there need not be contradictions between evaluations as there appear to be.

I take Socrates here to present a criterion for deciding whether x is good. He does argue on these pages also that pleasure is good but in arguing for that substantial thesis he makes use of an abstract pattern which could, it seems, potentially be applied also so as to assess different, i.e. non-hedonic, conceptions of intrinsic value (good, in my usage). So Socrates provides Protagoras with is a tool for making decisions about good.

What does Socrates mean to achieve by introducing this tool? Why does he not contrast his and Protagoras' values as they stand, without mapping them on to an abstract framework? If he did not use the framework then he would need to concede that he and Protagoras disagree. By using it, in turn, he can argue that their disagreement is merely apparent, not real. They are thinking imprecisely so they appear to disagree. But if they achieve the appropriate kind of focus then they can find that actually they agree.

Later in this essay, we will often be meeting with the idea that harmony is achieved by making ethics more precise. Its questions are to be more exact. Real results are attainable on this condition. Disagreements appear to arise in ethics but really in them subjects mix ethics with non-ethics. This is one underlying point about the function Socrates takes himself (or his criteria) to have.

Now let me note various aspects of what Socrates has been found so far to say.

First, his first criterion for good consists of an *evaluative thought experiment*. One is to imagine something and to evaluate it. He does this himself and he tells Protagoras to do the same. This is different from empirically perceiving an object, as imagining is unlike perceiving. Socrates is, we can say, for thought (and speech). Also, what he wants imagined he also wants evaluated. So his test does not consist simply of wondering what is possible. Rather, it consists of considering such possibilities that bear on value. So the thoughts are assessed, or the thinking itself is critical. One takes intellectual positions, pro and con.

More drastically, Socrates is saying that an evaluative thought experiment is to *settle* whether x is good. It has final authority. If pleasure turned out to be good, for example, then this would not be so because it is pleasing. So if someone were pleased, this would not show that pleasure is good. No, it needs to seem satisfactory in an evaluative thought experiment. This is the independent judge. Conversely, Socrates does not in my view ever indicate that if x satisfies his thought experiment then any further assessment of x is needed. For if x passes his test then that is all that needs to be said for x. One does not need additionally to consider whether x seems satisfactory also when practiced as a daily habit for a week, for example. Thought decides, once and for all. And the thought is of course not only Socrates' but also his interlocutor's.

All of Socrates' criteria in this book will consist of evaluative thought experiments, and the features noted in the preceding two paragraphs apply to them all.

Second, Socrates' first criterion consists above of pairing x, a candidate universal good such as pleasure, with *many different* other things and not only with specific ones. So one pairs x with y but also next with z and not y. For on the above pages there is pleasure taken in one thing and also in a very different thing, and the *only* constant between the things is their pleasingness.

This can be taken to mean that if x is good then x is "primitive." A primitive property is one which does not co-vary with any single other property in all worlds. Socrates seems to require this above in testing the value of x relationally to y and then to z and not y. Everything but x itself should be shifted, and in numerous ways, or x is not tested. (For *all* pleasures and *only* pleasures are good on his hedonist hypothesis.) If this could not be done for some x, i.e. if that x is not primitive, then apparently it could never qualify as good in Socrates' sense. It would not be testable in the way that he demands.

Let us pause here to note what this would mean. Primitive properties are entirely isolable from all other properties. Analytically, one checks whether a property is isolable from another by attempting to imagine the instantiation of the former without the latter. If there is any possible world in which this is the case, we have isolability between the two properties at issue. A property is primitive iff it is isolable from *every* other property.

Here are some illustrative examples. The property of being a tiger is not completely isolable if in every world that you have a tiger you also have an animal. If so, you cannot draw these properties apart from each other in your imagination. As another example, think of the property yellow. Perhaps there is nothing that all possible yellow things share beyond their being yellow. If so, this property is isolable (primitive). Pleasing things, again, may have nothing in common phenomenologically, for the pleasure taken in a musical may consist of a sound and no taste and the pleasure taken in one's favourite food may consist of a taste and no sound. If this indicates that "pleasure" stands for a heterogeneous set of objects (like "thing," perhaps "game") then it stands for no single property, and so it is not primitive. Pleasure is not complex in the consistent way that tigerhood is, one might say, so pleasure and tigerhood would fail of primitiveness in different ways.

Several questions can be raised about this kind of a test and about the above examples but these need not detain us now. For still in this chapter (1) the above analytical way of individuating candidates for good will be called into question. In chapters 2 and 3 individuation will no longer be analytical, and I will attribute this non-analytical way of thinking to Socrates. So we are first working on a false hypothesis.[2]

Third, Socrates wants objects not subjects separated. That is, we are not to place *ourselves* in any counterfactual context like a possible world. So we are not to ask ourselves whether we would appreciate pleasure even if we were e.g. pleased or in pain, but whether we do appreciate pleasure as *pleasure* is in different worlds. By contrast, Descartes in his *Meditations* asks whether x holds even if its thinker is insane or possessed by a demon. Here it is the epistemic agent who is tinkered with, not her thought-object. In Socrates one tinkers with the object, and the subject remains the same. I.e., Socrates seems to think that authoritative and non-authoritative views differ from each other not in any subjective way but objectively. Judges are not to be altered, and the objects they judge are. Authoritative parties hence concern themselves with *different things*, and to attain authority is to attain new topics and goals. Accordingly, we should not expect from Socrates accounts of ordinary topics or aims. For he wants to change topics. He wants to address precise questions about which there are no disagreements (not those vaguer ones on which people seem, even to themselves, to differ while actually discussing different topics under the same names).

Fourth, in the *Protagoras* Socrates actually never says that if x is good then x has value in *complete* isolation, or that its goodness is discovered by completely isolating it. For example, if pleasure is good then it does not follow, for him, that a world with *only* pleasure in it would have value. Rather, if pleasure is good then any world with whichever sorts of pleasing things but without any painful ones is valuable. But the likely effects of what will actually happen in such a world *are* to be ignored, we saw, so there is some isolation. It is to be considered in a causal vacuum, as it were. Also, the property good seemed to need to be primitive and hence isolable. But I want now to say that despite these points there is a sense in which the separation of good from other things that he calls for in the *Protagoras* is not extreme but moderate. It will be more extreme in the *Hippias Major* and the *Lysis* in chapters 2 and 3 below, for then good will be isolated more completely if not completely.

Fifth, Socrates wants us to find *only one* good. E.g. pleasure is not to be an aspect or part or example of good. It is to be identical to it. In other words, if pleasure=good, then there is no positive world which is not pleasing; and no world with pleasure, minus its consequences and minus its pains, is to have negative value.

Given these points, we can formalize Socrates' first criterion as follows. x is good iff $x+y>0$, on the conditions that (i) $x \neq y$ and (ii) $y=0$.[3] Here y is any part a world may have that is (i) non-identical to x and (ii) indifferent in value. x and y are in the same world. If any y can be found which satisfies these conditions such that $x+y$ is not positive, x is not good. (In a way this is simultaneously a test for primitiveness for if x has a part z or z a part x (in every world), then x and z will be in all the same worlds, so x versus z cannot be used straightaway to account for any property of those worlds.)

I have inserted condition (ii) for the following reasons. First, Socrates says that pleasure minus pain is good. So good has value as divorced from evils. (This Socrates said at 351 C, E.) To illustrate this, good is like health, not like medicine. It is not effective against disease. Rather, it is that which medicine is for (and without the opposite of which—disease—medicine is unneeded). Second, and as already noted, if y were positive, then x would not account for the positiveness of $x+y$. But clearly it is intended to. I.e., Socrates wants good captured, and exhaustively. As noted, he does not want merely a part or aspect or example of intrinsic value but the whole of it. (We need the whole map, as it were.) Hence, y is not positive. But we already noted why y is not negative either, hence $y=0$.

I inserted (i) for the following two reasons. First, in the *Protagoras* Socrates does not want the goodness of x judged in such a way that x is isolated from every non-x. So some non-x is to be related to x when the goodness of x is decided upon. Second, *any* (per (ii), null value) non-x must render the same result. Hence, y must be any non-x that satisfies (ii).

As a final observation in this section, notice that this test is negative because x has been shown to be good only once *every possible* y has been tried out but we can probably never reach a position in which we can claim to have surveyed every possible (non-negative) non-x (for *any* x). For it is difficult to call limits to possibilia. A y we have not yet considered can always turn up tomorrow, it seems. Due to this, we can say that at least in the *Protagoras* Socrates gives us means to discover that something is not good but never that it is good.

In sum of 1.1., good for Socrates is a kind of secret ingredient. Its presence converts any indifferent world into a positive one. It does not convert negative worlds. And there are no two ways to convert indifferent worlds into positive ones: it is always the same one.

1.2. Support from the *Hippias Major*

In the *Hippias Major* Socrates offers the same criterion as in the *Protagoras* but he also says more, as we will see in chapter 2. Explicitly, this dialogue discusses the nature of fineness (*kalon*). Any world which contains even the least bit of fineness (x) and something besides fineness (y) will have value—provided that y per se is not negative (or positive, as we must think, see 1.1.). ("Fineness" is now used as a synonym for "good," see 2.3.)

At 295C-D the same term (fineness) is applied to a wide variety of things, which would on the face of them seem to have rather little in common: a horse, a vessel, a law. This might lead us to suspect that Socrates is thinking of a term, as "good" is thought to be by Geach, or as "game" (*Spiel*) is for the later Wittgenstein, which is used for objects that do not have anything in common.

But 292D makes clear that not only is the same word used for a great variety of things, for those things also share some particular feature which makes them deserve that honorific term. So there is actually something there, consistently, which we need to find. In the same passage, Socrates also seems to refer to a single property, not to many properties, so he seems to have in mind a primitive property. Very different objects share the same property: a stone, a human, a god.

The primitiveness of goodness or fineness seems also to be claimed directly at 303C-D. Here it is said to be such that if x has it then so does each part of x. So goodness separates (divides) at least as far down as does anything that has it. Being two, say, does not attach to its parts taken separately, for the parts are each of them one, not two (301A-B).

But Socrates seems at 292D also to intend exclusiveness, for the single feature he is after is apparently to be common *and* specific to all of the cases (of fineness) at hand. It, and only it, is present in *all* valuable things that are complex but which contain no intrinsically negative elements. For here he says that the *same* fineness is present in every fine thing, be it a stone, a god, or a lesson. There are no two ways to bear this kind of value.

Chapters 2 and 3 will explain further how good relates to good things and how it differs from them. For the time being, all that matters is that the *Hippias Major* seems to require exclusiveness and primitiveness as the *Protagoras* does. So it is not an isolated idea for Socrates.

1.3. Support from the *Lysis*

In the *Lysis*, Socrates says that all agents aim at the same end. This end is one of doing what one wants, i.e. independence or happiness. It does not attach to as diverse objects as does fineness in the *Hippias Major*, for it is a special ability that experts manifest (at least in a rough way), and this ability cannot be manifested by just anything, e.g. a stone or a horse. Experts know to police their own desires and to achieve their own goals, and they can be relied on to define the scope of their expertise from within (see 3.2. below). Their other properties vary: some are cooks, others doctors, etc. It is their commonalities that make them good, however, and not their differences, and their differences seem to extend to everything except their goodness. But there is no other good. Hence, in the *Lysis*, too, Socrates affirms exclusiveness.

Thus at least three dialogues feature Socrates describing the criterion of exclusiveness: the *Protagoras* (1.1.), the *Hippias Major* (1.2.), and the *Lysis* (1.3.).

1.4. An Objection from Particularity

Now I turn to objections to Socrates as I have so far interpreted him. Each section will contain one or a short set that naturally belong together. The objections are in cursive and the replies to them are in straight text.

Socrates requires a definition of good but neglects that a defined object as he construes it is a universal which per se *does not carry value and that a bearer of value is a particular.*

To this background, Socrates should offer us more particular advice, for he is now not advising us about good. We need practical examples, not abstract rules, for value resides on the level of particulars not abstractions.

In reply, Socrates does not deny that value resides in particulars. For in the *Protagoras* and the *Hippias Major* he said that various different particulars are good or fine, e.g. a horse or a vessel. He is saying that the property that they need to have to qualify as good or fine must be the same in every case. So Socrates agrees, at least sometimes, that good is to be predicated of particulars.

Second, Socrates has reason not to discuss things on a more particular level. For this would be to sacrifice generality of scope, both in meaning and in relevance. For in different societies and at different times only some issues will seem understandable or problematic, and only some things count universally as solutions. That is, only some views will be acceptable irrespective of one's background. They are "teachable." Only they have authority. Socrates sees his own issues and criteria as pertaining to such a neutral area. For to him only what one might call pure ethics is teachable, and applied ethics is not. What evaluative issues qualify as solvable and why will be our issues throughout this essay. But little in Socrates would be plausible if we did not observe that he is a reformist. As explanations or analyses of ordinary values his views would be quite poor.

1.5. An Objection from Context-Sensitivity

Socrates enforces too closed a mind-set, for sometimes we learn about new aims through experience. An absolute and changeless barrier will only prohibit growth. For changes in values are sometimes for the better. Socrates is merely obsessed with precision and applies this abstract dogma in an area of life—ethics—to which it is not suited.

In reply, I want to present two practical problems that Socrates tailors his criterion to solve in the *Protagoras*. (There will be more of them in later chapters, i.e. 2 etc.) These are (i) inconsistency and (ii) the impossibility of deliberate preference.

(i) At *Protagoras* 356A-E Socrates says that we need to develop a consistent view of our aims or we will end up contradicting and prohibiting ourselves. On Monday one might work for x and on Tuesday against it and for it again on Wednesday, ensuring that in any case no long-term aim could be attained. We would then ourselves make sure that we cannot get what we want. For in this passage Socrates says that we need precision about aims so that we do not keep shifting our views about them.

What does this have to do with exclusiveness or primitiveness? In a rationally ideal scenario, a standard for telling between aims would be single in the sense of implying no indecision or contradiction in any context in which it is applied. Two distinct standards might conflict about some cases. A complex standard, again, will be ambiguous between at least two possible alternatives (at least if all complex wholes are contingent). But if so, then it makes sense for Socrates to require, as a means to consistency, not only that there be an exclusive standard but also that good is not complex, i.e. that it is primitive. But that is just what we saw him requiring in 1.1. In other words, if consistency is valuable, and if it is precisely exclusive and (hence) primitive conceptions of good that enable consistency, then all and only primitive things should be welcomed as goodness, everything else being equal.

If this is correct, Socrates' criterion is to be accepted because accepting it leads one to avoid a problem about practical reason. Practical agents have self-interested reason to seek to avoid such a problem. For they want whatever it is that they want. The way they can get it is by being clear about what they want. They need to embrace a second-order value of consistency. This way they will not shift between wanting x and not.

This basis for exclusiveness about good (consistency) is obviously conditional on our having or needing to have long-term goals at all. Having none such we might find one kind of satisfaction on Monday and entirely different ones on Tuesday and Wednesday. There would be no conflict because there would be no constant theme. Then requiring exclusiveness or primitiveness would be unnecessary for consistency, so consistency could be had without them. In this way, Socrates' first motive for seeking exclusiveness is weak.

This motive for exclusiveness is also conditional a further point, that of our needing to confront counter-factual alternatives. If we are not likely to meet with severe changes in desires—even if we have long-term goals—then it does not matter, one can argue, that we cannot distinguish our aims absolutely. If the conflicts that need solving are not drastic and different enough then good need not be exclusive or primitive. As a matter of fact one might get by quite consistently with rather blurred conceptions simply because one would never meet with radical conflicts. There might be only moderate conflicts and complex standards might suffice for their solving or there might be no conflicts at all. Having long-term goals does not necessarily involve them. So here is a second obstacle to basing exclusiveness on consistency. Socrates can justly be called a dogmatist unless he gives us better reasons to play by his rules.

These are issues that are so far left open. But here is a third one that is irrelevant and it should be noted why it is that. This would be that as a matter of psychological fact clarity about aims just may lack force in extinguishing hesitations or temptations when the latter are irrational. For perhaps e.g. an alcoholic will turn to drink no matter how obviously her alcoholism is reasoned against. Perhaps she needs treatment, e.g. a pill, and no argument. This is irrelevant because Socrates' position is not psychological. He does not discuss the human psyche or brain. He idealizes about practical reason. He says what we have reason to welcome, not that we can have it easily or even how exactly we can attain it. He articulates in what way we would recognize it if we came by it. Of course, such articulations will lack relevance in real life if the ideals they guide to are impossible to attain, so psychology does matter. But in my view Socrates does not mean to discuss it in requiring what he does of good or right. For *every* requirement he makes consists in my view of an evaluative thought-experiment. *None* is empirical, i.e. such as to discuss e.g. human nature. So we need to discuss the psychological issues independently of Socrates if they prove to be problematic. (My own view is that many philosophers exaggerate such scenarios and that human agents are well responsive to reasons in the great majority of cases. The problem is rather that good reasons are so rare. There is ample demand, little supply.)

(ii) At *Protagoras* 312C Hippocrates cannot identify who it is that he wants to be taught by, a "sophist." But then in what sense is he choosing to be instructed by one?, Socrates asks. Socrates may mean, I want to suggest, that unless Hippocrates is precise about his aim then Hippocrates is not for anything in particular.

However, this point is not specifically about particulars; it is deeper. Hippocrates has no position at all, no for and no against. He just does not want. For if he were for x versus y, then he would see x and y as distinct. Conversely, if he does not see x and y as distinct then it is rather silly of him to say that he is for x and against y. For presumably he cannot draw an evaluative barrier where he cannot draw any barrier at all. (Never mind for now whether in seeing a difference one would necessarily be able also to *communicate* that difference and whether the difference should be *real* and not only apparent.)

In the remainder of this essay, I will always find Socrates to demand precision on the positive side. So if one is for x and against y, evaluatively, then it is x that he wants one to be precise about. So one does not need to be clear about what one opposes. The more general idea is that there is a kind of clarity that is not only necessary but also sufficient of good things. This position will emerge gradually throughout this essay. (However, it is interpretively correct that sometimes Socrates demands precision about negativities also. I ignore these passages because I cannot see why he does so. Also, such passages are rare and never crucial. So when he is serious—and precise—about precision, he wants to apply it only to what he commends.)

If this is correct about *Protagoras* 312C, then perhaps it is equally correct about Socrates more broadly. For Socrates' questions concern values, aims. And about them he demands precision, in definitions. So he demands *precision about aims*, we can say, *every time* that he makes his characteristic move of asking for a definition of a value. *Why* does he think that precision about aims is needed? I am suggesting that he may think in general that responsible decisions demand this. If so, then he is primarily an advocate of responsible, conscious decision-making. For then precision has value because it enables this, not per se. On this view, Socrates is not simply a friend of logic or essences. He is a friend of free decision, and he needs his formal techniques to enable free decision. He is not trying to put a straight jacket on any deliberating agent, then, for rather he is freeing evaluations from the irrelevant and disturbing complexities that prohibit them from becoming focused and convinced.

At this point, it is necessary to see why precision about objects may be presupposed in free decisions. This is an evaluative question. The interpretive question whether Socrates ascribes to such a connection will not be pondered at this time. The general idea that Socrates wants ends that are intrinsically fixed so as to allow for fully responsible decisions will receive ample interpretive backing in chapter 3, and more vaguely already in chapter 2.

Here is an illustrative example of my own of the problem that decision-makers face if their ends are not clear-cut. Take it that Deng wants to spend a day in the country. These are the very words he uses when he expresses his aim to his friend who asks what Deng is doing buying a bus ticket and when, having been interrupted by a phone call from work, he reminds himself of what he was about to do. When he contemplates the aim, however, he imagines pictures and sounds, all of a quite indefinite nature. If he were asked to draw clear a barrier between his aim and what does not belong in it, he would have some difficulties. He has not thought so much about what should happen there. But therefore, Socrates would say, Deng does not have a distinct aim in view. He does not want anything definite, and indeed he is perhaps looking forward to *not* thinking deliberately, the very indefiniteness of the situation having much to do with why he wants to go to the country. He would be in a similar situation if he went to theatre to see a play of which he had never heard, or if he voted for a candidate at an election of which he had never heard. These are not examples of deliberate behaviour *because* their aims are so indefinite. Situations like this may contain value, but not deliberated value. This is the kind of thing that Socrates wants to communicate by advancing his criterion of exclusiveness.

Hippocrates at *Protagoras* 312C is not acting responsibly because he is not aware of what he is doing. It is not clear to him what he means to do or why. In fact, he does not seem to be acting in a fully intentional way at all. He has not voluntarily adopted his aim, we know, because he has not even looked at it. If he could take clear aim at it in broad daylight and hence welcome it in full consciousness then he could distinguish it from other things. So it is, on this view, not really dogmatic of Socrates to demand distinctness of good, for rather he is liberating his interlocutor in making this demand.

This same general idea can be reflected in inter-subjective cases. Picture that we find ourselves in late 18th century England and 1 says to 2 that women should be given suffrage, to which 2 responds, "What next, suffrage for apes?" 2's *reductio* will seem arbitrary, like a bad joke at most, if humans versus apes belong naturally to the same and relevant kind. But if this is not so, 2's rhetoric will have bite (as it did for many at that time, when natural boundaries were viewed differently than they are today), for 1's preferred barrier will in turn seem like an arbitrary preference (i.e., something formed due to the nature of 1, not of the objects judged, and hence objectively arbitrary). This is to illustrate why an argumentative context can require that we find a particularly natural (besides a relevant) location for a value. (How we should understand "natural" here will be discussed in chapters 2 and 3.)

As a third example, witness a case that Lawrence Kohlberg confronted in his empirical studies. He posed the following dilemma to Jack, 11 years old: Mr Heinz's wife is ill but Heinz cannot afford to purchase the drug that would cure her, and yet the druggist refuses to lower the price for him; should Heinz steal the drug? Jack says he should. Why?

For one thing, a human life is worth more than money, and if the druggist only makes $ 1000, he is still going to live, but if Heinz doesn't steal the drug, his wife is going to die. (Why is life worth more than money?) *Because the druggist can get a thousand dollars later from rich people with cancer, but Heinz can't get his wife again.* (Why not?) *Because people are all different and so you couldn't get Heinz's wife again.*[4]

Jack finds that one choice is natural as the alternatives are, as it were, kinds apart. The two alternatives do not properly rank even on the same scale, as one ranks so clearly above the other, and due to its intrinsic nature. For money is generic and replaceable but Heinz's wife is not; but what is replaceable is better sacrificed simply because qua replaceable it is possible to replace, so its annihilation is not eternal but temporary.

Numerous analogical cases can be thought up, as they are familiar from daily decision-making. In everyday life the examples are not usually as drastic as the above, perhaps, because deliberations or debates may not be pursued to their deserved limits due to external pressures: many people do not find the time to argue for long enough periods of time, the energy to care, or the faith that things can be advanced. Conflicts are not only not solved but often they do not even receive expression. Compromises often take the place of conclusive arguments, as agents settle for merely getting by. But in moderate form, examples of the above kinds of regress arguments in ethics are probably familiar to most, and examples of them are probably many and different.

As a final point in this section (1.5.), is Socrates not exaggerating in saying that objects must be nothing less than primitive to qualify as chosen in full consciousness? (Would not e.g. organic wholes be clear enough, if they were organic enough?) It is difficult to say based on the *Protagoras* why Socrates wants to go this far. But the *Hippias Major* and the *Lysis*, discussed in chapters 2 and 3 below, will offer a basis for this. This is that the intrinsic features of good things must justify their goodness, and I will take this to imply that the decisive feature must in every case be a primitive one (or else it is not properly intrinsic).

1.6. Objections from the Autonomy of Ethics

There are many ways in which Socrates can seem to confuse descriptive with evaluative questions.

First, the decision whether x is primitive is not an evaluative one. It is metaphysical, scientific, or conceptual (or what have you) but it is not evaluative. Hence, it is not a decision to be made by a practical, evaluative party. So if deliberating agents must secure that what they view as good is primitive then their evaluations need to be confined from without by a non-evaluative authority.

Second, ethics is concerned with deeds not thoughts, and with desires not beliefs. One is moved to act by wanting something, not by any assertive state. But Socrates appears to treat ethics as just another descriptive discipline. For he says that good is primitive. But to agree that good is so and so is not per se to want anything. Simply describing good or intrinsic value may not connect at all with any desires.

Third, whether or not x is primitive, this does not decide the issue whether x has intrinsic value. Primitiveness is obviously not sufficient for intrinsic value: e.g. basic concepts or categories (or what have you) may be primitive but per se they are hardly common and specific to things that have intrinsic value.

Fourth, it may be correct that x cannot be sought in full deliberateness unless x is primitive and therefore stable in meaning and distinct from other things. But this is to impose an unnatural standard on evaluations. For evaluations are by their nature not clear. Their objects qua desired are ambiguous. The data of significant experience is complex, unclear, lively. To require conceptual rigor is to stand opposed to value. Accordingly, perhaps deliberate choices are never made if rigor excludes value.

The generalization is that Socrates wants to control ethics from outside ethics. If so, one does not have reason to submit to such control from an ethical point of view. So despite the points in 1.4. and 1.5. Socrates really does argue as a metaphysician, an analyst, or a scientist, not as a liberator.

We will see in chapters 2 and 3 that Socrates does not mean to require descriptive rigor. Good is to be primitive not descriptively but functionally (teleologically, ethically). Also, it is dynamic. So Socrates is an advocate of the autonomy of ethics in his own way. He merely does not succeed in saying everything relevant to this in every dialogue, e.g. the *Protagoras*.

But he definitely denies that value or good is necessarily ambiguous. So value may be entirely identifiable form a practical viewpoint and it may be dynamic in nature—this far Socrates is prepared to go—but it is not necessarily imprecise.

1.7. Summary

In this chapter (1) we saw that in the *Protagoras* Socrates presents a criterion for good which requires "exclusiveness" (1.1.). (This seemed to imply primitiveness.) It is found also in the *Hippias Major* (1.2.) and the *Lysis* (1.3.). It faces some objections that it is powerless against, but not as many as may at first seem (1.4.-1.6.).

Notes

1. If it is correct that Socrates premises on egoism then one can ask how he relates or might relate to an interlocutor who does not. I will not ponder this point anywhere below but I will do so briefly now.

As a first possibility, Socrates might meet with a *community* of speakers who viewed their interest as communally represented. It would not matter to Socrates if his interlocutor claimed to represent a community, but he would object if he had to discuss things with several individuals at once. Why? In my view, he never answers this question quite clearly.

A further possibility would be that his interlocutor would not claim to satisfy *anyone's* desires by identifying good in the way that she does. Such an interlocutor would want to identify good as being a certain way whether or not anyone wants or has reason to want it to be that way. Socrates never meets with an interlocutor like this. He meets with evaluative agents only. Everyone he meets contemplates plans of action. Not one wants to know simply how things are.

It is difficult to say what he would say *if* he met with the above kind of (non-evaluative) speaker. Possibly, he would deny that they are speaking of the same topics at all, for he is after what one has reason to want (what one benefits from).

Sometimes Plato (early, middle, or late) is taken to represent the preceding kind of impractical view in the epistemology of ethics, in my view falsely. He is not describing a reality beyond desire but a high-point in desire (or desirability). This does bring him to reflect on reality, but not in a way that would by-pass practical interests.

2. The analytical hypothesis is false normatively about ethics *and* interpretively about Socrates if the view I advocate of both (ethics and Socrates) is correct. For per se the *Protagoras* is merely *ambiguous* about how we are to individuate, e.g. analytically or evaluatively. So it could just as well premise on analysis or evaluation (or something else). But we should not say that it errs by premising on analysis if it does not explicitly premise on it. Hence the errors we will find in the analytical view will be our interpretive ones and not Socrates' normative ones. None the less I will sometimes speak of the *Protagoras*' view as erring for the sake of simplicity. As noted in the Introduction, the alternative would have been to use more complex phrases.

3. In using "+" I do not mean that x and y must have degrees of the same quantity of anything nor hence that good is quantitative for Socrates. (Perhaps it is in the *Protagoras*—this is not my issue because at any rate Socratic good is not quantitative in the dialogues that I will discuss in chapter 3, so quantitativeness is not an element in his stable and serious position.) I mean rather that x has value despite the presence of y. It might have been less misleading to write not "x+y" but "x and y" or even "x but y."

4. Quoted in Gilligan p. 26.

Chapter 2

GOOD IN THE *HIPPIAS MAJOR*

In the *Hippias Major*, Socrates advances a different criterion of good than he did in chapter 1. This time he says that x is good if x is self-evidently good. More exactly, he says that if x is good (or fine) then x is both a general measure of good (fineness) and what is found to be the best (finest) thing by using that measure. x is to be both at once, even one thing qua the other.

This is one way to "self-predicate" something.[1] In what might loosely be called the standard sense, to self-predicate is to predicate something of a predicate, or to apply a property to itself.[2] An illustrative example would be "Largeness is large." But I will view self-predication as a predication of a predication, so that a predicate applies to an *act* of predicating. An act that picks itself out is self-predicated. Also, I will say that the acts Socrates has in mind do not merely predicate something of themselves in an evaluatively neutral sense, for they do not merely describe anything but rather they applaud or prescribe what they concern. They themselves (superlatively) satisfy these requirements that they make. So they are, one might say, "performatively" ("pragmatically") self-satisfying. (They are not merely self-*consistent*, as "I am a liar" is not and "I am an apple" is. The latter locution is not an apple.)

I will begin this chapter (2) by presenting an "analytical" view of self-predication which I oppose (2.1.). Then I sketch the evaluative view of it that I favour (2.2.). In this section (2.2.) I also relate the *Hippias Major*'s criterion of good with the *Protagoras*' (discussed in chapter 1). In 2.3. I offer the interpretive basis for the evaluative reading and in 2.4. I explain in what sense the *Gorgias* seems to support it also.

I will try to clarify Socrates' meaning in 2.5. by comparing him with Heraclitus and some of his other predecessors. I will say that Socrates develops his predecessors' conceptual frames into what is more general and reduced.

In 2.6. I present an objection to the *Hippias Major*'s criterion of good. This is offered by Socrates himself in the *Lysis*. He will reply to it in the same dialogue, which is discussed here in chapter 3.

2.1. Analytical Self-Predication

An easily arrived at problem about the *Hippias Major* is as follows. In it Socrates asserts a doctrine which has been called "self-predication." According to it, the measure for fineness (good) is itself the finest (i.e. best) thing. This seems problematic because we do not usually attribute intrinsic value to standards but rather to particular things. A standard per se is, after all, not of special value; it needs to be put to use. A standard as it stands is not usually viewed as its own use. But on the other hand a particular thing cannot seemingly be a standard. One reason to think that it cannot is that if it is then it is left unclear how anything but that particular can satisfy the standard; for then it seems that that other particular can at most resemble the first, in which case we are left wondering what resemblance is. A standard seems to need to be other than a particular or its satisfaction seems to need to be a matter of mere vague, unexplained, resemblance. Hence the question arises what Socrates might mean. Two quite different interpretations of his meaning are the "analytical" and the "evaluative." I present the former and its problems in this section (2.1.).

An analytical reading of Socrates' meaning in self-predicating is that good is a primitive universal and that ordinary, apparently good things are non-primitive (for complex) particulars that have that universal. These particulars are not-good in the sense of having too many properties. They do not have only the property good. They have other properties also. But all things which are not identical to the universal good are not good things at all. That is, ordinary good things are not *identical* to (the universal) good but they are perfect enough *instances* of good. So the analyst does not contradict everyday intuitions about what is good. She only exposes the specific property that good things share. Analysts of this sort are often called "metaethicians," since Moore's time. The analytical reading of Socrates says that Socrates is an analyst.

The evaluative reading that I will favor is as follows. A normative relation when directed at that same relation (or, really, that same relat*ing*) is good. That same relation when directed at things other than itself renders those other things apparently or somewhat (not really or fully) good. To illustrate, take it that being pleased about something is the relation or relating that is to qualify as good. Then one should be especially pleased about being pleased. Being pleased about being drunk should not be *as pleasing* (i.e., as satisfactory of the relation). So good is a normative relation directed at itself. It is not simply some primitive property or other. And the distinction between universals and particulars is not really relevant at all, contrary to the analyst. I will explain these connections and connect further points to them in 2.2. But this will do as a first sketch.

The analyst has Socrates saying four more or less absurd things:

(a) that a universal is a good thing, so a universal is an instance (i.e., as if Socrates simply did not realize that he is doing metaethics not normative ethics),
(b) that a primitive property is self-evidently anything at all (for in the *Hippias Major* Socrates claims that good things are self-evidently good),
(c) that what makes a thing self-evidently good is the property of being primitive (as if that were a sufficient explanation of Socrates' meaning), and
(d) that having a property which another thing does not have is the same thing as not having any further property (for in the *Hippias Major* Socrates says that ordinary good things relate to ordinary non-good things as does good proper to ordinary good things).

(a) If the analytical reading is correct, then Socrates confuses universals with particulars, for on the analytical interpretation Socrates mistakenly says that the universal, good, is itself an instance of good. This is a confusion because a universal is not an instance.[3] But this is not charitable for then Socrates is guilty of an elementary mistake.

(b) Being primitive is not at all like being self-evident but as we will see the *Hippias Major* means to demand self-evidence; hence it cannot mean primitiveness or Socrates is confused (which is again something we would rather avoid thinking). This is because a primitive property is per se not even *about* anything. So how could it be *for* anything, e.g. for a thesis that something is so and so, or that something should be so and so? One might of course say that a primitive property can be *used*, and perhaps with special clarity, as evidence for something. But this is very different from saying that the object at issue itself draws the relevant connection. For if it is *we* who draw it and not the object, then we will have done a part of the epistemic work. Perhaps, then, the same object would do different work in someone else's hands and disputes would arise between the disagreeing interpreters. Primitiveness per se does not rule this out. It leaves things too blank. It cannot do the kind of work that Socrates wants done.

(c) If primitiveness made an object good, then all primitive things would be good. For example, such an apparently primitive thing as the colour yellow would be good. But surely it is not (see 1.6.). Again a lack or charity is the problem.

(d) In the *Hippias Major* Socrates repeatedly says that fineness proper differs from ordinary fine things in the same way as ordinary fine things differ from non-fine things, see 2.3. But the analytic reading says the former difference is different from the latter. For the analyst says that ordinary fine things have a property P which non-fine things lack and fineness proper has no property other than P. But not having P and having some property other than P are not the same thing. This is the plain interpretive error of attributing to Socrates a view which he repeatedly contradicts.

(a)-(d) are reasons to oppose the analytical reading of the *Hippias Major*. But these are only weak and inconclusive reasons for preferring the evaluative reading unless we can see that the evaluative reading faces less problems than does the analytical one. For of course it could turn out that even though the analytical reading faces severe problems, the evaluative one faces different ones that are even worse. I will next advertise the advantages of the evaluative reading (in 2.2.).

2.2. Evaluative Self-Predication

In this section (2.2.) I will (i) briefly present the general idea of the evaluative reading of the *Hippias Major* on self-predication, (ii) note in what way this criterion relates to the criterion described in chapter 1, and (iii) explain Socrates' likely motive or motives to self-predicate.

(i) It seems contrary to Socrates' intentions to predicate good of anything but a particular. The problem is to say how a particular can be a measure for any particular or for particulars in general. This, anyway, seems like one way to try to unravel the issue.

But now, what particular can possibly measure itself or others? A candidate for this role is some *act* of measuring. An act is a particular event in time and it may also be a relation to other things. This relation can have a certain scope. It is not easy to picture such a scope being general without linguistic expression, and this brings us to consider *speech* acts in particular as potential bearers of good. Normative and general ones are *prescriptions*. One can prescribe, "X!"

How is there a self-relation to this background? One answer is to say that the act of prescribing ("X!") obeys that same prescription. If so, the content of X is not the same thing as the act of prescribing it, but the prescriptive act can itself *satisfy* X, and that is a point we can fasten on. A banal example is to command: "Command!" Given that saying this is to command, to say it is simultaneously to obey what one says. In such a case one practices what one preaches, and by doing one and the same thing. Despite this, recall, the prescribed content is not identical to the act of prescribing it. The relation is one of satisfaction, not of identity.

As a next step, we need to recall that the prescriptive act is to be the only proper thing to satisfy its content in some sense. For good is besides a measure, the *best* instance on that measure. It is not just any instance but the superlative one. This is what the *Hippias Major* will be found to say in 2.3.

One thing this cannot mean for Socrates is that the prescription is the *only* possible thing to satisfy itself. For he predicates good of things other than good proper, not only of it. There are e.g. good (fine) horses and pots in the *Hippias Major*, as we will see. But also, mere *possibility* cannot be his meaning either, for if it were then nothing would distinguish good proper from good horses and pots, but clearly he intends these things to stand a class apart from each other. How, then, is a prescriptive act to be the best case of its own satisfaction? Not based on any logical, analytical consideration, I am saying.

One alternative (perhaps not the only one) is to go for the throat: a prescriptive act may be the evaluatively superior instance of its own content in a sense *that that content specifies*. I.e., the prescription, "X!," would be satisfied best by that prescribing act, and the answer to the question in what sense this satisfaction would be "best" would be: X must tell us this or X (or its prescription) is not self-evident.

To illustrate this without any claim to ethical seriousness, fearing might be especially fearsome (or the only really fearsome thing, as F.D. Roosevelt claimed). If it is, this relation would turn to itself, because that would be where it finds satisfaction in the sense that it itself specifies. (In the prescriptive mode one would need to speak here of fearing and scaring occurring at once because fearing is passive. Someone would then say "Fear!" or "Boo!" loudly and surprisingly enough and react with fear.)

(ii) In the *Protagoras*, discussed in chapter 1, Socrates seemed to say that good is exclusive, and this we took to imply primitiveness. We also saw that his procedure was inductive and negative. In the *Hippias Major*, he seems on the evaluative reading to relate to these positions as follows.

Let us look at primitiveness first. It seems impossible for anything to self-relate evaluatively without its being primitive. For if the relation is complex then every time it relates to itself it relates to something else as well. But then it is never satisfied specifically by itself. In this way, we can think that self-predicated things are necessarily primitive, so if one can secure that x is self-predicated then one need not additionally and secondly make sure that it is primitive also.

But if the good are to obey only the prescriptions they themselves make, and they depend as above on primitiveness, *and* if their characteristic relations are evaluative, then seemingly primitiveness needs to be possible to secure from an evaluative point of view. We need to ponder whether this is possible. If it is not then we cannot say that the evaluative reading of the *Hippias Major* really is charitable. But if it is then not only the coherence of that interpretation has been assured, for then some of the objections in 1.6. will also not apply against the Socrates. In this case there would seemingly be progress in normative plausibility. For if one can identify an end as a normatively self-predicated one without additionally considering whether it is primitive from a descriptive (non-evaluative) point of view then evaluations need not be tied down from without. For then there is such a thing as ethical specificness, a specifically ethical kind of precision.

But how would this work? Let us look again to fearing for the sake of illustration. If a fearing agent fears only fearings and nothing else then this may secure that fearing is primitive. She would simply not react at all to other things, let us say. (This is an oversimplification, for in Socrates' actual position there are also somewhat or apparently good things, not only properly good ones and non-good ones; see 2.3. and 2.5.) One could present her with darkness and with sudden noizes, for example, and she would be unshaken. The most diverse kinds of fearing, however, would each of them elicit her characteristic response.

This may sound far-fetched. But consider what would be involved. Now one would individuate good *by being good*. For if fearing were good (because only fear would be fearsome) then by fearing (being good) one would indicate, by one's relations to fearsome things, how good is individuated. For one would relate only to what is common and specific to fearings. So individuation would emerge from within the evaluative point of view.

If this is to work then it should never occur that some non-fearing party would find several commonalities in all of the things that the fearing fear. The fearless should not see any commonalities except by beginning to fear also. I.e., the relevant level of individuation should not be accessible without exhibiting the appropriate normative relation to things. The interpretive claim that Socrates believes in an ethical level individuation will receive more support in chapter 3.[4]

Next, let us look at exclusiveness. It does not seem to connect with self-predication. For if x satisfies itself it does not follow that some y does not also (and x≠y). To illustrate, perhaps fearing is fearsome and loving is lovable. Fearing may not be lovable nor loving fearsome. Each of these evaluative relations would then satisfy itself and deny each other, but both of them would beg the question against each other. (This is hardly surprising because self-predication seems like a requirement of specificness in a relation, but exclusiveness stands for scope, and one does not attain scope by becoming specific.)

I the remainder of this essay I will largely ignore exclusiveness because in my view Socrates does not tell us how to decide whether anything is exclusive. In 1.1, I noted that he does give us an inductive route for determining that x is *not* exclusive, but the *Hippias Major* clearly opposes an inductive procedure, as we will soon see, so we cannot view this dialogue as following that lead.

Now let us turn to a final aspect which separates Socrates' criterion of good in chapter 1 from the evaluatively self-predicated one. In chapter 1, good was to be discovered by imagining various possible cases of it (e.g. of pleasure) and by noting what is common and specific to them. The cases were different complex particulars.

In the *Hippias Major* Socrates favours a different order. It is not an inductive one. For first we need an ideal instance which simultaneously provides us with a primitive universal. Only secondly can we come to apply this universal to non-ideal cases (such as pots and horses). And clearly Socrates is not much interested in performing this second step at all, for his impatient insistence is constantly on the need of the ideal case.

This can seem like a major change of mind. In one dialogue one advanced inductively and in another this procedure is opposed. But we already also noted above that evaluative self-predication seems to imply primitiveness, and this is to say that there appears to be continuity. Moreover, all the while his topic seems to be intrinsic value (in the passages that I discuss in chapters 1-3).

(iii) Why would one want to avoid an inductive procedure in identifying good? An obvious reason would be terminability: non-inductively good might actually be identified conclusively at some point. Clearly this should be preferable in anyone's view, at least given that it is at all possible. For without clear-cut answers every evaluation will have to be accompanied with a "perhaps," and nothing can be properly wanted or fastened on or ranked above alternatives. Our wills would then not be properly exercised, and decisions would be left to the winds (*to the degree* that they are left insecure, at least).

But the preceding is not a reason to say that a *perfect instance* of good needs to be found. For inductiveness might be avoided simply by picking out the universal, good, without considering a potential infinitude of its instances first. Then all one would do next is apply the universal. Why not go this way?

The *Hippias Major* does not seem to me to contain a clear answer to this question. It suggests a rather imperfect one, however. This is that good things terminate debates (intra- and inter-subjective ones) but that an uninstantiated universal would not do this. It would not do this, one can think, because it seems possible to identify a universal, and to take a favourable attitude to its use as a standard, and yet to be blind to just how it is to be applied. For example, one might state that one is for courage without being able to identify cases of courage or without being courageous in taking the position in question. If this occurred then application issues would be left open, and then good things could not be identified automatically after having identified a universal, good. But this would in a sense mean once again that debates are not terminated. (For one would have the laws but one would not know how to apply them.)

Two things are wrong with this motive, however. The first is that the *Hippias Major* does not seem to contain any explicitly pragmatic view of good. For it does not actually say that good things must practice what they preach (or realize what they prefer, etc.). It does want to make ethical debates terminable, but this may not bring one directly to pragmatics in Socrates' mind. The second problem is that the above is not a reason why good things should be *perfect* instances of standards they invoke. It is only a reason why they should be instances of standards they invoke. So it does not lead one to the kind of paradigmatic role that Socrates seems to want the good to have in the *Hippias Major* (according to the evaluative reading).

Despite these problems, it seems to be charitable to view the *Hippias Major*'s doctrine pragmatically and hence to say that only the second of the problems described in the preceding paragraph applies to this interpretation. For the pragmatic reading of the dialogue's intent renders the dialogue more consistent than at least one easily imaginable competitor, the analytical one. Thus I will argue in 2.3. If this is correct, then this dialogue should be taken pragmatically. But then the kind of terminability that Socrates is after in this work should also be thought of as potentially pragmatic. For if on the one hand he says that terminability is to be sought—and this is beyond doubt (see 2.3.)—

and on the other hand he offers a pragmatic criterion of good then it may well be that he views terminability pragmatically. Indeed, it may then even be implausible to deny that he does.

However, this should not leave the reader satisfied, for the above is an insecure strategy in interpretation. More secure will be what we will be found in chapter 3. (Then the above problems will covered in the following ways. In the *Lysis*, Socrates says that instances of good must guide us forward to future and better instances (of the same kinds they themselves belong to) or they cannot intrinsically satisfy. So instances and standards cannot be separate or there is no satisfaction because there are no intrinsically guided processes. The reason why good things must be perfect instances is a little different: in the *Lysis* Socrates says that instances must police standards, not standards instances, or the instances are not self-sufficient. But if they are not self-sufficient then nor hence are they intrinsically satisfactory. An act of revising a standard is, paradoxically, to satisfy that standard especially well. It is such standards that are fitted to the good. This idea will be clearer in chapter 3.)

2.3. The Interpretive Basis

In the *Hippias Major*, Socrates obviously means that what is "fine" (*kalon*) ought to exist. Many different things are fine, e.g., fine horses and fine pots, so many different things ought to exist.

But "fineness itself" is the finest thing (289B-C). It is special at least in that it is not discovered to be the finest one by comparing it with other things, for rather one can identify other fine things only by using it is a reference point (289C-D). A maiden, say, can qualify as somewhat fine (289B-C), but only once fineness proper has first been found.

So the object Socrates wants to know about is both a single superlative instance on a general standard and a general standard itself. It has two roles at once, we are to think, because Socrates does not mean hereby to inquire simultaneously into two distinct things. He nowhere distinguishes these aspects in this dialogue. In other words, what is finest is a/the measure for fineness (good).

This can be taken to suggest that what he is after is self-evidently fine. For now the same x that provides evidence of fineness is itself the finest thing, so perhaps the thing warrants itself.

But in thinking thus we are assuming that fineness itself applies at all to itself. Perhaps it applies only to other things, qua general standard, and somehow receives its superlative status due to this function. This appearance is contradicted by Socrates' seeming desire to find in fineness itself something self-evident (286C-D, 291C-D). But if what he is after is (i) a general standard, (ii) a superlative instance (on some standard or not), and (iii) self-evident then it seems rather fitting to think that what he is after is self-relational. For perhaps it is (iii) *qua* being (i) and (ii) at once. This, at least, is one way to see Socrates as a sensible speaker. For then we can say that he is not making various different demands (for (i), (ii), (iii)) but rather a single one, consistently and with reasoned focus.

But why is self-evidence needed? What does Socrates himself actually say about this matter in this dialogue? At 304B-E Socrates repeats that an absolute standard or case is presupposed in other judgements about fineness. He does not say that it is *probable* that Hippias' or other agents' pre-critical intuitions *will* be questioned in any way that makes it necessary for them to respond with any claim about self-evidence. He is rather saying that the very possibility that they can be should lead them to seek self-evidence. But why?

At 304B-E Socrates seems actually to say that *talking* about fineness should be embarrassing if that talk is not based in self-evident knowledge. More specifically, claiming or teaching should be backed up with what is self-evident. One should not correct others without it or claim authority or organize things in public life. Socrates may mean that claims need to be made not only by those who happen to wish to teach others, like Hippias, but also by agents who may not have that aim, e.g. Thrasymachus, for at 304B-E he seems to describe a kind of intra-subjective debate. It is as if one needed to make self-evident claims or one could not convince one*self* either. The idea would then not be that one would not predictably happen to convince oneself sometimes, just as it was not in the inter-subjective scenario, but that the convincing would not be explicit enough to qualify as voluntary. This Socrates *may* mean, and that is all I wish to claim at this point.

Next I want to invoke some interpretive evidence against the analytical reading of the *Hippias Major* described in 2.1. First, we should notice that Socrates does not seem to view fineness as simply being *instantiated* in somewhat or apparently good things but rather as their origin (292C-D).[5] If so, then this supports the evaluative reading against the analytical one because on the former good things *actually change* things or at least our views of them. They would not simply be present in somewhat good things as parts or aspects.

But this is a weak claim because Socrates does not actually theorize the relation between good things and somewhat good ones in this passage or dialogue. He gives no analogies in relation to which we could perceive his meaning. All we have is a few phrases and nothing structured. Hence we should not contend that this relation is vital to Socrates' serious position. If it mattered in his economy, he would theorize it by invoking analogies.

But here is a second point that seems firmer. At e.g. 289B-C Socrates is clearly after an instance of fineness, as already noted, and this is against the analytical view. Hippias' error seems not to be that he gives examples of fine things but that his examples are not of unambiguously fine things. So Hippias is to give a description of something that is fine and not of an uninstantiated universal. Socrates wants to know to what the term fineness or fine *applies*, not what it *means*, so he is pursuing substantial ethics not metaethics.

Third, we already noted that in this dialogue Socrates seeks what is self-evident but that the analytical reading did not capture this, see 2.1. Fourth, at 289B-D he says that ordinary fine things relate to non-fine ones as the fine proper relates to ordinary fine things, which the analyst frankly denied, see 2.1. I will return to this analogy between three classes of objects in 2.5.

In sum of 2.3., I do not think it can be doubted that in the *Hippias Major* Socrates wants ends identified simultaneously with measures that pick them out. Also he seems unambiguously to demand ends like this from deliberate authorities. However, the claim that he has in mind intra- and not only inter-subjective authority can still seem speculative. But I will be returning to it amply still in this essay.

2.4. Support from the *Gorgias*

The *Gorgias* features Callicles claiming that naturally more powerful individuals should receive more rewards than their less able fellows. Socrates draws that Callicles cannot plausibly mean something this simple, for two persons have more physical power than one, so by Callicles' definition two persons are better than one (489D). This is not what Callicles means by praising power. He means to praise powerful individuals, not masses that can subordinate them. Socrates means to show that Callicles' view *cannot* be clearly defined, and that due to this it is not a serious, authoritative position for at anyone at all, provided they perceive it for what it is. I.e., *nobody* would affirm a view like Callicles' *if* they only saw its content.

But in exposing conceptions of good for what they are, what does Socrates reveal about them? How does he do it? In regard to Callicles' hypothesis, Socrates is puzzled not only about *who* (or what) is supposed to receive more than others but also *what* they are to receive more *of* based on Callicles' idea. For he asks Callicles whether the best weaver should have the largest coat and the shoemaker might have the greatest number of shoes (490D-491A). Socrates is, of course, ridiculing Callicles. But he is serious that Callicles must identify both things at once, for they go naturally together. If x deserves y, then both x and y demand identification. Moreover, x and y must somehow match each other. It is as if the intrinsic nature of x already dictated what y needs to be. In other words, he requires that good is self-relational. One is to reap what one sows, to receive what one produces. This connection is drawn by Socrates, not Callicles. Callicles' thought is not like this. For him, some deserve a larger share of all goods even if their own nature is not generative of all of the goods at issue. For he seems to mean that the physically strong justly get to rob others of all kinds of goods. So one might say that for Callicles but not for Socrates there is a type of currency for exchanges in general, such that this currency is not sensitive to variations in the goods exchanged.

But it would be incorrect to represent Socrates' and Callicles' positions merely as two competing conceptions of good. Rather, Socrates does not actually say what is good in the *Gorgias*. He lays down a pattern for its identification. It is in relation to this pattern (criterion) that views of good are revealed for what they are. If they are views about intrinsic value at all then they must conform to this pattern. Good is self-relational and Callicles must merely say what good is. But he is not allowed to say that x is good though x is not self-relational. The self-relational pattern is not something Callicles is allowed to be for or against. He must give an answer that conforms to it. If he does not see why, explanations can be given. He does not qualify as an authoritative judge of good without submitting to it.

Thus interpreted, the *Gorgias*' criterion of good is quite similar to that of the *Hippias Major* above. Both dialogues say that good is self-relational.

But these two dialogues can also seem to differ somewhat concerning good, for the *Gorgias* appears nowhere to say that the point of requiring a self-relation is to ensure that good is self-evident. The relation in it (in e.g. the above quote) seems rather to be only productive. But there was a causal aspect also in the relation that the *Hippias Major* required in 2.3., for what is properly fine gave fineness to things. It made them have that property. But it was also self-evident. In this way, the *Hippias Major* perhaps represents a more developed and more specific view of good than the *Gorgias*. But we will not find Socrates explaining why he makes both causal and epistemological demands until chapter 3.

As against this, it might be said that Socrates does not prescribe the use of a self-relational pattern in the *Gorgias*. For he may think that the good do not deserve more of anything than do the bad. On this view, the good would not be out for rewards at all. They would in fact not want much of anything. Rather, they would oversee distributions. They would command e.g. that things are to be distributed according to need (490B-C). The good would be judges, as it were, who want nothing for themselves. They would serve the general public. Accordingly, we find Socrates praising besides impartiality (ibid.) also ascetism. Satisfaction is for the ascetic a matter of not wanting anything, not of attaining much. One is to exercise control inter-subjectively and intra-subjectively but for the sake of nothing.

But the above cannot be Socrates serious position because it receives a lethal objection: if the desireless are fortunate then stones and the dead are fortunate (492E). But the dead do not seem more satisfied or fulfilled. That one does not have desires does not make one happy. Rather, satisfaction is attained through action, or self-sufficiency. So here Socrates seems misled in his conception of good. Accordingly, his praise of ascetism and impartiality are only hypothetical. They are not views that Plato wants to present as authoritative. Otherwise he would not present an objection to them. Or at least he would give Socrates some sort of a reply against Callicles' objection. But he does not, and Socrates concedes the point, for he says that Callicles is correct on the above point against Socrates (492E).

2.5. Socrates and Heraclitus

We can formalize Socrates' criterion of good in the *Hippias Major* somewhat as a revision of what Fraenkel calls Heraclitus' "thought pattern." That pattern is:

> (A) aRb=bRc. (Or: a<b<c.) Example: an ape (or child) relates to a man as a man does to a god.

Here a and b are ordinary particulars. In relation to them, R is somewhat definite, and based on R c is also. But "god" (i.e. c) and R are not made more explicit than this. Only a and b are explicit. To this Socrates adds that R=c, so his pattern is:

> (B) aRb=bRR. (Or a<b<<.) I.e., the measure of fineness itself is the finest thing.

Socrates simplifies Heraclitus' pattern in this way. Of course (B) is an outlandish pattern per se but the difference between (A) and (B) does seem to be the difference between the two philosophers' patterns, and this difference is now my topic.

In (B), the measure is the end. I have said that this should be taken to mean that an evaluative relation is to be both a standard for individuating things *in* evaluating them *and* something which satisfies that same relation perfectly. In contrast, Heraclitus does not seem to mean that his *god* teaches of herself or himself. Heraclitus stands between his god and lesser-valued things such as children and apes, as a man, and it is in this status that he teaches of god. For Socrates this would be unacceptable because now the god would be submitted to a man's (Heraclitus') standard. (Socrates might quip, "Heraclitus, would you say that you, a man, are well identified by a child?") For standard-setting itself is the Socratic goal.

Besides being more reduced, Socrates' pattern differs from Heraclitus' in its use. For Socrates uses his to pose questions to which he wants answers, whereas Heraclitus is content to suggest implicit answers. Socrates demands activity from his hearers and does not let them go easily.

The important similarity between Heraclitus' and Socrates' patterns is that ordinary particulars can on both patterns be invoked to communicate what is not familiar from everyday life. The trick is that R applies in the same way to both pairs, (a,b) and (b,c). The motive for doing this may also be similar for both, for probably both use a pattern so that they can communicate not only non-ordinary but also abstract contents. These should have general validity (and perhaps general reality[6]). Ordinary objects or ordinary universals would not be abstract or general enough. R is something that is praised as decisively relevant, and R is a quite generally applicable relation (though it applies perfectly only to what is non-ordinary). Its generality for both seems to have something to do with its being praiseworthy. I am not sure that Heraclitus means his god to be primitive, but perhaps he means something in that direction if he can point towards god by invoking various enough examples in using (A).

According to e.g. Snell (chapter 9), we find patterns in still earlier Greek thought also. One might formalize one of them as follows:

(C) aRb=cRd. E.g., an army in defence (i.e. a) relates to an attacking army (b) just as does a rocky shore (c) to recurrent pressures of ocean waves (d).

(C) is found in Homer according to Snell (pp. 200-201), but the formalization is mine. R is again general and praised. (Probably it is something like persistence, unyieldingness.) As a matter of historical fact, perhaps (A) is developed from (C) and (B) very much seems, as noted, to be a merely more reduced version of (A). (Less developed still are simple comparisons like "Love is (like) a rose," etc.)

It is also perhaps worth noting that the *Protagoras'* criterion of good actually resembles (C), for in that dialogue a single relation (of e.g. being more pleasing than) is said to convey intrinsic value no matter what its instantiation. So one could potentially fill in an infinite number of pairs of examples beyond (a,b) and (c,d), e.g. (e,f), and R would none the less remain the same in content and at least as authoritative as before (perhaps more authoritative given that the inductive generalization has a firmer basis the more several examples support it).

2.6. An Objection from the Paradox of the Will

At Lysis *220B-E Socrates introduces a paradox which at first sight seems to deny that anything can actually be good. For he says that if we were in need of nothing then nothing would be of use to us.*

Socrates seems to mean (among other things) that if we attained what is perfect in the sense of leaving nothing to be desired then we would no longer desire it (e.g. to attain it). But we do not ordinarily think that we would not appreciate what we aim for once we attain it. On the contrary, we aim at the things we aim at because we think we will appreciate them when we have attained them, not only when we have not yet attained them.

If this paradox is valid, we seem to need to choose between two alternative conceptions of good. It is either something we desire but do not have or something we have but do not desire.

But it could of course also be that the paradox is not valid. For example, one might argue that one can appreciate a perfect thing even when one has attained it, and even if it leaves nothing to be desired, just as one can appreciate e.g. a painting without wanting anything further in relation to it, e.g. to own it or to prolong one's contacts with it. One may simply marvel at it. But this example is irrelevant, for what would be relevant is rather the following. One wants to see the painting and once one gets to see it one's desire to see it is satisfied and gone. What one appreciates in the painting beyond this point in time is not what one aimed at. If, again, one's aim is to marvel at the painting and not merely to arrive on the scene to see it, this aim is attained only once the marvelling begins. But then one need no longer desire to marvel at it, as one already is marvelling at it. So qua sought for end marvelling is just like any other end and the paradox applies. Once we attain what we want we have no more reason to want it because we already have it.

Here is a second counter-example. Can one not desire even what one has, namely to keep it? Is this not a case of wanting something that one already has? No, for if we desire to keep x then our desire is not satisfied when we attain x but only once we get to keep x. So this is not a case where one desires what one has. For it is not a case in which one's desire has been met.

But this paradox applies to good as Socrates viewed it in the Hippias Major. *For if one attained a self-evidently good thing then that thing would leave one with nothing to desire. So one could desire it only when not having attained it. (If one desired it still when having attained it one would have to be unaware that one has attained it. But no one would be* for *ends of this kind, i.e. for ones which consist of error.)*

This objection will be replied to in 3.1.-3.2.

2.7. Summary

In this chapter (2) we saw some reasons to read the *Hippias Major* in an "evaluative" as opposed an "analytical" way (2.1.-2.3.). The *Gorgias* contained similar ideas (2.4.). So did Heraclitus, to a lesser extent (2.5.). Finally, we met with Socrates' own objection to himself (2.6.).

Notes

1. We do find "self-predication" also in the *Protagoras* (330C; "justice is just"), but this passage does not in my view tie in well with that dialogue's view of good as this was discussed in chapter 1. More generally, every time Socrates self-predicates he is not necessarily saying something plausible in my view.

For a full list of passages in which Plato self-predicates explicitly, see Wedberg. This list does not contain the passages of the *Lysis* that I view as self-predicating in chapter 3 below, however.

The early Platonic dialogues are also full of more playful expressions of self-predication: e.g. in the *Laches* (193E) Socrates says that he and his interlocutors must exhibit endurance so that they can come to recognize endurance. (So they need themselves to exhibit what they study in studying what they do.) This is a playful expression because it is only a brief note. It is not used as a standard for assessing views systematically. Self-predicated expressions of this playful kind are so frequent in Plato that some interpreters have been led to view his philosophy as "enacted rather than asserted" (Press p. 33) in the dialogues. To them it is as if the praised properties (endurance, good, etc.) found instantiation in the Platonic procedure of philosophizing. I believe the relevant properties to be always asserted and partly enacted.

2. It is to speak rather roughly to say that there is any agreed on standard sense to self-predication, however, for diverse interpretations have been offered of the passages in which Plato or Socrates seems to self-predicate. For some alternatives, see Nehamas.

3. It is not relevant at present to say that a lower-order property (yellow) can be an instance of a higher-order one (color) because even the former would be a non-particular and seemingly no one would view any non-particular as bearing intrinsic value. Hence I ignore this possibility here.

4. On the normative side, this position could be discussed at much more length. Such a discussion would not involve much reference to Socrates, however, because he does not seem to be troubled by the idea that things might be individuated evaluatively (teleologically, functionally). This is not to say that he should be. But many recent philosophers are.

Perhaps the area of philosophy in which similar issues are most discussed today is the philosophy of mind. Diverse functionalisms are surveyed by Rey. Functionalists in this area of philosophy think that mental things share not material but functional features. Materially they admit of different realizations, e.g. synthetic and organic ones, but their functional roles are constant. The functions are at least usually viewed as causal. Whether they are also thought of as normative depends on the functionalist.

In ethics, noncognitivists (like Stevenson and Hare) hold that ethical properties are not empirical but pragmatic (expressive, prescriptive), so they are individuated on a different level from empirical things. But typically noncognitivists see this as a reason to view ethical properties as unreal. This is definitely a departure from Socrates' position. In contrast, functionalists about mind often assert the reality of functions.

5. A single passage, 294D-E, might even be thought to show that Socrates at least sometimes ranks metaphysical issues above epistemological ones, and hence that he does not view these two areas as identical or inter-related. He could then be inquiring what causes fineness whether or not that causation is recognizable. For in that passage he asks Hippias whether a given feature ("appropriateness") makes x be or appear fine. In the latter case x would appear fine without really being so, he says. Yet this choice between *false* appearance and reality arises only because Hippias has said at 294A that appropriateness makes things seem but not be fine. The dichotomy arises only due to this hypothesis of Hippias', and it is drawn nowhere else in the dialogue. But Socrates does not approve of this hypothesis, so he is really protesting against identifying fineness with anything that makes things appear other than they are. Hence, it is misled to think that Socrates is mainly a non-epistemological metaphysician in this passage. I.e., even here his interest is not explanatory.

6. In what sense is reality at issue? Compare Sartre p. 3: "The reality of that cup is that it is there and it is *not me* (...) the series of its appearances is bound by a principle which does not depend on my whim." If the thing interprets and communicates itself, as in Socrates though not in Heraclitus, then these tasks are not left to others. It is then not up to those others to make of it what they wish, so it is "real." It is independent of them.

Chapter 3

GOOD IN THE *LYSIS*

In the *Lysis*, Socrates' framework is rather different from what it was in chapters 1 and 2. In general, this dialogue discusses such things as teleology, functions, efficient causes, and purposes. In contrast, the *Protagoras* and the *Hippias Major* can appear at first sight to think rather in terms of formal causes (than final or efficient ones). So are these dialogues really about the same things? My view is that they are. They are all concerned with intrinsic value (good), among other things. But do they agree with each other about it? I will argue that in the *Lysis* Socrates presents a third criterion of good which is independent of and superior to his earlier two (in chapters 1 and 2). This third criterion is that good things need to be viewed as self-sufficient in a certain sense.

Self-sufficient things as Socrates describes them are ends that are their own means. Think now of evaluative relations which are satisfied when self-applied, as in chapter 2, but which thereby *change*, develop, what they relate to (i.e. themselves). For some evaluative relations do change what they concern or fail utterly to apply. This may sound puzzling at first. But this seems to be Socrates' recipe for avoiding the paradox of the will presented in 2.6.

I will begin in 3.1. by articulating my interpretation of the *Lysis* on good without an interpretive basis. I offer that basis in 3.2. In 3.3. I explain in what senses Socrates' third criterion seems independent from and superior to his earlier two criteria in 1 and 2. It solves more problems than they do without being more complex than they are.

In 3.4.-3.6. I offer support for *Lysis*' view of good from three other dialogues: the *Ion*, the *Hippias Minor*, and the *Cratylus*. Each is unambiguously supportive of the *Lysis*, I claim, but none of these three dialogues addresses all of the points that the *Lysis* connects. In my view, the *Lysis* contains Socrates' most developed view of good.

In 3.7. I explain why Socrates' objections to the possibility of self-rule in the *Charmides* are not relevant at this point. They concern right not good, i.e. external (policing, controlling) relations versus internal (productive, revealing) ones.

In 3.8. and 3.9. I consider some objections to the *Lysis*' view of good. They try to point out what is confused, interpretively and normatively, about self-relations if these are understood as in the *Lysis*. However, these objections appear to misunderstand Socrates so they are not reasons to think he errs.

3.1. Causal, Epistemic, Ethical

In this section (3.1.) I will present my interpretation of Socrates' view of good in the *Lysis*. According to it x is a good thing only if (i) x is a desire which causes a further desire y such that y is logically independent of x, (ii) x is a standard for the identification of y, and (iii) x views y as an end. (The first relation is causal, the second epistemological, and the third ethical.) After going through these points I will provide some examples of my own design for what Socrates seems to have in mind. (All of them will be imperfect, but they should be structurally informative.)

(i) The paradox of the will says that if one is or has x then one has no reason to desire to be or have x. This is not to say that such a desire is impossible, but rather that such a desire would lack any point. It is practically unreasonable—something one should not want whether or not one does.

Here is a final and banal illustration of the paradox of the will to ensure that it is understood. Take it that you want to own a particular painting. If you already do own it then you have no reason any longer to want to own it. You may want to *keep* owning it, but that desire is not the same one as the first. The *first* desire was already satisfied, *it* has become pointless. If, in turn, you want to own the particular painting for as long as you live then your desire is not met when you purchase it. It is met only if you possess it for as long as you live. But if you possess it for as long as you live, then you no longer have reason to want to possess it for as long as you live because you already do.

How then can anything intrinsically satisfy? This is the question the paradox is really meant to raise. In the *Lysis* Socrates praises self-sufficiency as good. He means to praise, among other things, a productivity. x is good only if x causes y and x and y are logically independent. x must have power. I.e. x must be active. x must generate something outside of itself.

But perhaps there is something odd about viewing productive states as *ends*. Most of us are accustomed to appreciating effectiveness in means, not in ends. But Socrates means, in my view, that the self-sufficient are ends which are effective in generating further ends. In other words, teleological end-points do not terminate causal chains but initiate them. (They are "unmoved movers.") Ends are to be viewed as intrinsically of such a nature as to generate further ends.

This appears to be a way to avoid the paradox of the will. When an end is attained, that end by itself generates a further and independent end. When that independent end is attained, it in turn should generate a still further and independent end. We should desire chains of this sort because this conception of ends allows us to escape the paradox of the will.[1]

A few potentially troublesome implications of this view of good need now to be noted. The first is that if the causes now meant are intentional then Socrates seems to propagate a particular sort of *dis*satisfaction. For if the causes involved are desires and one should desire effectiveness then one should desire desiring. But the paradox of the will said that desiring implies dissatisfaction, for it is pointless (or ill informed) to desire what one has. One ought to desire only what one does not have. Hence, one ought, in a sense, to desire to desire only what one does not have. In other words, one ought to welcome dissatisfaction. But this can sound implausible. For surely dissatisfaction is not an aim. Dissatisfaction does not satisfy. But in response to this complaint it must be observed that the self-sufficient as Socrates describes them are effective at bringing about the changes they desire. So it is not really dissatisfaction that he means to welcome but effective action which happens also to involve temporary dissatisfaction.[2]

A second troublesome implication can seem to emerge as follows. What is now initially desired when a causal chain of the relevant sort begins cannot be its end-point but its first step. For if the end-point were desired, then its beginning would not be viewed as an end. But in that case *ends* would not breed further ends so we would fall by the paradox of the will. So we are to see only the first link in the chain as an end. The later links in the chain cannot be in sight—or they, not the first link, would be viewed as ends. But then it follows that the later links in the chain will not be chosen by us as ends. But then we could not be said to be making a rational decision at all in welcoming them (compare chapter 1). It is as if we had to travel in a tunnel (not seeing far before us) but also should not. This is a problem that I will address again in 3.9. Call it the "tunnel problem."[3]

(ii) In the *Lysis* the good need no extrinsic guidance. So they are not only causally independent (in initiating chains, as in (i) above) but also epistemologically. But Socrates conflates these aspects, the causal and the epistemological, in the case of the good. So if we picture a causal chain from x to y to z, then x should not only be a means to y but also say why y in particular deserves to be an effect. Likewise y for z. Each step along the way *teaches* one about the next step. So each step is not only effective in producing the next step but also a lesson about what the next step should be.

In this dialogue, then, these two relations, the causal and the epistemological, are not separated from each other, so it is as if x were a standard of y *qua* effective of y. One way in which this should not sound unattractive is as follows. Some kind of a desire might suit both roles. For given that the causes at issue are intentional, they are desires (or at least contain them). But desires can fit the epistemological role also, ultimately rendering something self-evident. For it is now the self-evidence *of intrinsically valuable things* that is at issue. If x does not desire (i.e., have a favourable attitude to) y, then x does not say that y has value. If x were simply a description of or an indifferent thought about y then x would not be evidence for the *value* of y. In this way, it is natural to predicate self-evident goodness of x only if x is (or contains) some desire or other. Drawing these connections is far from establishing that epistemological and causal relations can ever be identified with each other, of course. But it goes some way towards showing that perhaps there is a class of things—namely certain desires—which are both evidence of goodness and effective of goodness. It is they that seem suited to the epistemological role, at least.

(iii) As a point that is independent of what I will find Socrates to say in 3.2., the causal chain from x to y to z would ideally be one of increasing satisfaction. For the lessons learned in an ideal process would each of them be steps forward, not backward or level. The lessons would grow in significance. So not only should x cause y and y z (as in (i)), and not only should x instruct one (or x) about y and y about z (as in (ii)), for it should also be the case that z>y>x (and x>0). Otherwise the chain is not progressive but regressive or repetitive (on an evaluative scale).

Socrates does not actually seem to speak of ethically progressive chains like this in the *Lysis* or elsewhere, but we can take him to mean them none the less. His chain at *Lysis* 219B-220B does feature z (the final end) rating above y but both y and x seem to have null value. A father values wine (y) because it will cure his son (z), and he values a jar in which the wine is (x) (219D-E). The jar and the wine do not matter to the father per se. The jar matters only for the sake of the wine but even the wine does not matter for its own sake. They are only means, not ends. (So, intrinsically speaking, x=0 and y=0.) But we know, I will argue in 3.2., that he views the good as self-sufficient. If this is to be a solution to the paradox of the will then x and y must have more than null value, for if they have null value then the chain from x to z is not a chain of ends.[4]

(i-iii) speak of three different relations but the *Lysis* does not draw them apart. How can we picture all three relations obtaining at once? I.e., how can we view them as Socrates seems to view them? What can he mean? Here are some independent reflections about this.

Consider Hanna, 17, who wishes to become a medical doctor. Having only limited knowledge of biology or medical practices she has an undeveloped image of what it means to be an active doctor. She wishes to "effectively help" "people" (she says) but she is aware that only studies of medicine will tell her how she must view things ("helping," "people") and how she must affect them to actually be effective. She begins her studies and in the process learns that she is most interested in oncology and so she begins to specialize in that field at 25. At 32 she is a practicing specialist and her work consists of constant lessons, via practical professional experience as well as through studies of journal articles. In this process, Hanna constantly specifies her aim. She learns more about it. She also becomes more and more effective (let us assume). She herself changes (qua deliberate agent) as her reasons develop into more effective, authoritative, and satisfactory ones. This process is triple in Socrates' sense: earlier states cause later ones, measure them, and rank below them. But the connection between early and late states is not logical but causal and one of discovery, so the process is transformative. It is an effective chain of progressive (for more rewarding to Hanna) re-definitions of good. Hanna does not, after all, *analyze* "people" or "helping"; instead, she makes discoveries about her aim in a causal process.

This chain is too complex to suit Socrates' criterion literally, for it involves e.g. social networking and empirical information. It fails of distinctness. Another failing in it is that it does not directly involve any evolution in an activity because directly a medical doctor causes health, not any advance in her own activity. This second shortcoming is apparent in a different way in a second example of a craft, shoemaking. Shoemaking produces shoes so if there were shoemaking about shoemaking then shoemaking would need to be revised *by* (in) producing a shoe (or a pair of them). The shoe would stand out as a paradigm instance. Perhaps exact replicas of the shoe could be manufactured. But the shoe would not make them. Moreover, the future shoes would always be only replicas, not advances, and the shoe would not tell us how to make advances. (It might guide us to replica at most.) Due to these reasons, the paradox of the will would not be avoided by shoemaking.

Now let us move away from the crafts and inspect some evaluative self-relations.

If *loving* were a good relation in the *Lysis*' sense then any time that one would properly love one would change, develop that relation itself. Loving would not merely alter loved ones (i.e. loved particulars), as it would be the case if the loved responded with love to their being loved. Rather the relation of loving itself should be transformed in the process. Probably loving is not like this because it seems to transform particulars (loved ones) at most, so loving is probably not an example of a good relation. So it does not seem like the kind of desire that we could identify as good because it lacks the developmental aspect. But perhaps its failure would not be due to any lack of distinctness (which was the problem with medicine and shoemaking).[5]

As a second example consider lying, as if someone said "Lying is art" (meaning that they are identical). Perhaps to lie about something is to alter it and it is also a normative relation. If this locution is very much a lie then perhaps it is self-relational in the required sense. But notice that if the content of the locution is correct then it is no lie, so the statement must be false. Accordingly, being a lie it cannot be art either or the statement is true (because then at least sometimes lying *is* art) and not a lie. But hence the *next* step in this process (lying about lying about lying) would be impossible to make because it would be art about art and it would thereby *not* concern lying (if the first locution, that lying is art, is indeed a lie).

As a third and seemingly more suitable example, consider truth-telling. It could be that telling the truth *about* telling the truth is an especially suitable way to satisfy the command "Tell the truth!" In contrast, it would not be—so one could argue—very revealing or honest in any deeper sense to expose more particular truths, e.g. that one lied at some particular time in the past. But truth-telling seems in every case to reveal and hence in a sense to change something, so if it is about itself (the relation of truth-telling) then apparently its revelation is about itself (that same relation). One might admit e.g. that sincerity is just thinly concealed self-importance (thereby implying that one is being self-important). This claim would not have to be e.g. original but only true to perhaps qualify as more sincere than e.g. any confession about one's past intentions. If so, it would be at least a rough example of good in the *Lysis*' terms. For it seems like a first order evaluative relation (a desire) which transforms itself when directed at itself, and the transformation seems especially satisfactory of the relation in question.

Structurally this example seems successful because it might be used to form a patterned process: on Monday there would be sincerity about sincerity ("It is self-importance"); on Tuesday there would be sincerity about sincerity about sincerity ("Self-importance is x," and this locution would have to be especially self-important). In contrast with this, we just saw a few paragraphs ago that no continual process was possible for lying. But the failure of the present example is another: nobody would rank self-importance above sincerity, so the chain sketched above would not be ethically progressive. (So truth-telling should be revealed as something other than self-importance.)

We might look at still further ordinary evaluative relations and check if they qualify. The checking in every case would consist of asking, for x, whether (i) only x in particular satisfies x and whether (ii) x satisfies x by altering x. x would of course not be satisfied by anything if it were not *for* something in the first place. But if it were satisfied well by x in particular then arguably x would necessarily be distinct. And yet if it were transformative of itself qua satisfying of itself then seemingly it would be a developmental process. In Socratic spirit, I leave the imagining of more positive examples to the reader.[6]

3.2. Interpretive Backing for 3.1.

I have made claims about Socrates' view of good in chapter 2 and just now in 3.1. for which I did not provide interpretive backing. Now is the time to provide that backing.

Socrates notes to Lysis how paradoxical it is that, on the one hand, his parents wish him to be happy but, on the other, they subordinate his will to that of a slave (208C). His parents dictate that he must obey a slave. The appearance of paradox arises because happiness is defined as doing what one wants (207D-E, 208E). Hence, Lysis is prohibited from doing what he wants by those who want him to do what he wants.

Strictly, this is of course no paradox, for it is possible (e.g.) that Lysis' parents believe or know it to be instrumental to his happiness that he is for a time unhappy, e.g. until he acquires certain abilities. For he cannot do what he wants without those abilities. He may not be able to bring about the ends he wants and/or he may want things that do not really serve his self-interest in some sense. This is exactly what Socrates is driving at by presenting his paradox

(209A-210D). So, as usual, he presents his paradox for a pedagogical purpose. It is not really a paradox, for there is a way out of it. (That Socrates' interlocutor finds that way is one goal of the exercise.)

Next Socrates observes that provided that one succeeds in convincing another that one has the relevant abilities, one will be allowed to do as one wishes. An acknowledged cook is allowed to throw handfuls of salt into a dish whereas whoever is not an acknowledged cook will be denied the right to throw in even a little (209D-E). Likewise, if one passes for a doctor one can sprinkle ashes into a person's eyes (210A), and of course unqualified persons are not allowed to do this.

These examples illustrate that as an expert one will (be felt to) qualify as the best judge as to what belongs to her area of expertise. So the scope of each area of expertise is defined from within, by the experts themselves. The cook and the doctor themselves define what it is appropriate for a cook or a doctor to do.

In Socrates' terms, experts thus defined are "happy." For they themselves get to define what they should or should not do. They themselves have—nay: are—this authority. But in young Lysis' case, we do not find this identity relation. What is not identical is on the one hand Lysis' desires and on the other authorities that tell him what he ought or ought not to do.

But not only the identity of an epistemic standard with a first-order desire is asserted in these passages. A causal relation is intended also. This is because a slave not only judges things on Lysis' behalf but also affects them to Lysis' benefit. In the same way, cooks and doctors do not only judge things, they also change things; they produce food and health.

This is enough to show that Socrates means to *identify* expert sanctions with the desires that experts can happen to have. For otherwise he would not say that only a cook is allowed to identify the bounds of cooking or a doctor of medicine. He would not have chosen the above dramatic examples if he did not mean identity.

Against this it might be said that Socrates does not intend an identity relation but rather one in which expert second-order desires police first-order ones. Accordingly, he would mean that good is complex, containing expert and non-expert parts, not partless, as it would be were the relation (between some desire and good) one of identity. This interpretation can be argued based on the causal (not the epistemic) features of Socrates' examples: the active subject, the cook, is other than the means of the action (vegetables, knives, etc.). Likewise with the doctor: her means include medicaments, and her actions are not identical to these. So Socrates' examples feature complex things as good.

But these examples are not to be taken literally. For in so far as Socrates himself aims to provide Lysis and his friends with happiness, he does a bad job at it if it is crafts such as cookery and medicine that provide them with it. For he is not a great cook or doctor. For his kit of tools is not like the cook's or the doctor's. What he teaches is formal and normative. For his issues in this dialogue concern, broadly, the structure of the desiring relation. Most notably, are desiring subject and desired object similar or dissimilar? The pro's and con's of both views are studied by viewing their implications. The question is, besides formal, normative, so that Lysis and his friends are brought to do things as one should. The formal implications studied are teleological: if like loved like, would both be *satisfied*? Would like *have reason to* love like? Or if opposites attract, is this more *satisfactory* for the parties involved? Do such relations make purposive sense? This is the general nature of Socrates' thought in this dialogue. Things are individuated by their functional roles, so that they are opposed in nature iff their functions are opposed (which is when e.g. x is satisfied by what leaves y dissatisfied). But he means to *cause* happiness (good) by these intellectual means. But then what he views as causes are not like causes in cooking or medicine. Therefore, the analogy between his own craft and cookery or medicine cannot be strict. Hence it is misled to view them as implying that good is complex. Complexity need not be one of the analogical properties intended. For we have just seen that some of the properties of the analogues are *not* relevant.

But, next, there *is* reason to think that Socrates is attempting to provide his young interlocutors with at least some degree of happiness. If he did not, he would not have them think through the things he says, but rather he would advise them directly to study crafts. Philosophical reflection would be unnecessary if it did not contribute to self-sufficiency.

But this leaves open the option that for Socrates philosophy is but a preliminary in the process of becoming happy. Perhaps it is not the only or even the main part of that process. But Socrates absolutely never actually advises anybody to study a craft. The things he invokes about them are familiar to people already. Indeed, this is why he invokes them: they form a basis of analogies by which he can illustrate some of his meanings. And yet he tries to provoke absolutely everyone to philosophy, and with no immoderate ambition. His questions are broad in scope, and so are his various hypotheses about them. He appears to think his broad and bold questions answerable. (In general, his reliance on the powers of the human intellect seems great.) So he seems to think philosophy not only necessary but also sufficient for his aims. But he says, we already saw, that self-sufficiency is good, so that appears as his aim. Hence, he does seem to think that it is precisely philosophy, formal and normative, that is instrumental to good. But therefore analogies with cooking and medicine should not be taken as exact. Only some aspects of those crafts are relevant, and only approximately. What is relevant is the appropriate self-relation, but not due to its complexity.

This view finds support in the *Apology*. As a normative philosopher, Socrates believes himself to be living the examined life which provides him with the best things humanly attainable (20D-E, 21B-22E, 29D-31A). Hence, his aim does not require the use of means extrinsic to normative philosophizing. He believes these to be a sufficient cause of the attainment of good. (I will return to this aspect of the *Apology* in chapter 6 when discussing right.)

I have three further reasons in support of the identity view.

First, his examples show that in his view expertise grants a person liberties; it does not provide her with restrictions. For she may e.g. throw handfuls of salt into a dish. She may do things that are not commonly associated with cookery.

(It strikes non-cooks as not expert-like to throw handfuls of salt into a dish or to put ashes into a person's eyes. This is why Socrates invokes these examples.) She may redefine the scope of that craft, at will. So it is not that her first-order desires obey her second-order ones, but rather conversely: that the former get to select the latter. That is, she may do and rule as she happens to please. Her expertise provides her with a right to this, but with no obligations. She need not meet external constraints, and this is why she can do things that strike the non-expert as non-expert-like. (I ignore for simplicity the prospect that an expert might misuse her status and hence be justifiably deprived of it. For the decisive issue is really what qualifies one as an expert in his favoured sense. I am also ignoring for now, but only for now, that for Socrates expert knowledge is necessarily teachable and that hence experts' actions and verdicts cannot *ultimately* seem odd to non-experts. 3.4. and 3.5. will point to further aspects of how good experts stand out in communication. We already surveyed some of these in 2.2. and 2.5.)

Second, his definition of happiness shows that he must mean identity. For if the relation were not one of identity, it would not be one of happiness by the above definition. For the happy are not policed from without as Lysis is, he says (see above). But if one is policed by a craft, one is policed from without (unless one—or specifically one's desire—is identical to the craft). The craft cannot stand above the desiring. For if it did, the craft would stand to first-order desire as a parent or slave does to Lysis, and this is clearly pictured as an unhappy state above.

Third, in the *Lysis* the object and subject of friendship are repeatedly conflated, so that "is a friend to" (se e.g. 222D) can mean either something that likes or something that is liked—or indeed both, simultaneously. We can choose here between, on the one hand, attributing to Socrates a very elementary error of confusing two senses of friendship and, on the other, viewing him as suggesting, and driving the discussion towards, his desired conclusion—that desire and desired, or lover and loved, should be one and the same thing—right from the start, by setting up the question in such a way that his answer to it will seem natural. But the former alternative seems extreme, for surely Socrates is aware that the two senses of friendship are distinct. Indeed, we *know* that he is, for he thematizes that difference by considering the possibility that what is loved does not love the lover in return (see 215B-C). If he were guilty of the error of confusing these meanings, it would be impossible for him to say this. It is hence far more plausible to think that he conflates lover and loved so as to suggest that in the best (but not in all) cases they are one and the same thing. In other words, good does not contain a lover and a loved but is both at once.

Given these points, good must be partless for Socrates.

3.3. Relations between the Three Criteria

If there are developmental self-relations and it is these that Socrates has in mind in the *Lysis* then seemingly he now avoids the problems that his earlier criteria in chapters 1 and 2 were built to avoid but without suffering from their shortcomings.

The criterion of this chapter (3), self-sufficiency, solves the problem of chapter 1 if this third criterion requires distinctness of good things. It does this if causally self-relational things are distinct. Good things on this third criterion would perhaps be distinct as activities that concern their own kind of activity specifically. But the specificity would not be descriptive. It would be developmental, for the good would specify their crafts by bringing these into fruition.

This third criterion also solves the problem described in chapter 2 if it connects standards and aims intrinsically. Now the standards (or their uses, i.e. standardizations) cause the aims but are not (descriptively, non-teleologically) identical to them. They do not simply return to themselves as aims. They produce them. But this is not merely to repeat them so the paradox of the will is avoided.

This is all rather "iffy." *Are* there ever causally, productively, distinct acts or not? Iff there are then we can view Socrates as presenting not a series of criteria of good but a single one. Then we would not need to use several steps in a procedure. We would also not need to decide, impossibly, between two options each of which satisfies a different criterion but neither more several ones than the other. I am sorry to have to say that I cannot claim Socrates to show that there are distinct productive relations, but seemingly we have several reasons to say that he needs them. So if his program is tenable then his test for whether x is good consists of a single step. (I.e., does x develop x or not?)

3.4. Support from the *Ion*

In the *Ion* Socrates says a number of things that can be viewed as supportive of the view of good he seemed to affirm in the *Lysis* earlier in his chapter (3). I will first (i) present these supporting points and then (ii) give reasons why some objections to this view of the *Ion* should not be accepted.

(i) The issue in this dialogue is whether Ion, a rhapsodist, qualifies as an expert and why. The larger issue behind this one is the nature of expertise in any area, i.e. not specifically about poetry.

Is a discussion of expertise inevitably a discussion about good? Experts are productive of valuable things, Socrates says (537C). This is not to say that any or all experts produce good, for perhaps they produce things of mere instrumental value, or perhaps in the *Ion* Socrates means to discuss a species of value of a different sort (for instance right, or something else). We do not know this directly from his views in this dialogue. In this sense, we cannot use the *Ion*'s views as supportive directly of any doctrine of good.

But there is ample evidence of a more indirect sort. It is not indirect in the sense of being tacit or difficult to understand. It is explicit and definite. Rather, it is indirect in that the topic of the *Ion*, expertise, is something with causal and epistemic powers which the *Lysis* predicated of the good. Certain idealized experts have these powers in the *Ion*. It is in connecting causal and epistemological powers that the *Ion* agrees with the *Lysis*, not in connecting either with good. Here are three particular features the *Ion* attributes to experts.

First, experts form first links in causal chains. They initiate such chains and are not mere later links in them, effects (533D-E). Nor are they without causal involvement. Socrates means hereby to contrast expertise with servitude (534C-D). Experts rule, causally speaking. They move things and are not moved by other things. This is one thing the *Lysis* said about the good.[7]

Second, each area of expertise is distinct from others by virtue of its topic (537D). Socrates means by this also that no topic is addressed by two different areas of expertise, so topics of areas of expertise do not overlap. They do not e.g. concern the same objects on different levels of generality, and they do not concern different aspects of the same things. What one knows through one art one does not know through another. So two experts from divergent fields cannot know *any* of the things the other knows.

This does not imply that the aim of each area of expertise is primitive because they could each concern non-overlapping complex objects. But it does imply that Socrates' own discussion of expertise, discussing other areas as it does, is not per se within an area of expertise (*if* he discusses not only various areas of expertise but also their topics, which he does). Is he then no expert? He nowhere says that he is in this dialogue. But we do know that if he were one then his talk of expertise in general could be a mere lead-up to his actual expert's work. This is the view that I favoured in 3.2.

Why, however, ought we to accept that no topic is discussed by two distinct areas of expertise? Socrates can be taken to be discussing epistemological autonomy. If e.g. a medical doctor really should be listed to in a conclusive way about topic x then one should not need additionally to consult an arithmetician also, and nor should the doctor. If, conversely, the arithmetician has authority to correct the doctor then the doctor cannot herself be a conclusive authority nor hence an expert in this strong sense. But this implies that if there is an ethical expertise then that field is epistemologically autonomous, which is just how that field was viewed in earlier sections of this chapter (3, and also in 2). On this view ethicians have their own objects and principles of individuation. If so, their objects are not e.g. naturalistic (i.e. such as to depend on the natural sciences, e.g. the medical science of Socrates' day or ours). In the *Ion* Socrates is implying this same view though he is not asserting that there is an ethical expertise. He implies that if there were one, then it would be epistemologically autonomous. It would not be concerned with the objects of other crafts.

Are these assertions, the first for the causal self-sufficiency of experts and the second for their epistemological autonomy, correct about the crafts of Socrates' day? Apparently not, for e.g. a medical doctor would seem to be corrigible by an arithmetician. Ordinary crafts seem to overlap. Hence we should not view Socrates' views on expertise as descriptive of such crafts. They are rational idealizations, best-case scenarios. They should be realized even if they have not been.

Third, experts provide more than positive commentary of their objects. In other words, their range of topics is broader than the range of things they affirm or finally aim at (530D-532B). For example, an arithmetician picks out not only valid calculations but also invalid ones (531E). So she does not comment only perfect calculations and leave invalid ones ignored just as she ignores e.g. trees which do not even attempt to calculate anything.[8]

(ii) One could say that the *Ion* provides interpretive evidence against the view of good advanced in 3.1.-3.2. above, for one can say that in the *Ion* it is not e.g. lovers who say what is worth loving (or what love is) because in it Socrates opposes individuation from evaluative points of view. For Ion is not in his right mind—deliberate and active—when he makes his characteristic presentations before his audiences. For e.g. when presenting what is fearsome he is afraid (535B-E). Socrates is now viewing this as a *fault*, not as a merit.

Socrates can seem here to be saying that it is not e.g. lovers who should teach of love but certain impartial, cool-headed agents who do not get carried away by their topics. If he means this, he is against teleological individuation.

He could mean this also in telling Ion, as he did in (i) above, that Ion must be capable of commenting failed attempts at good poetry or Ion is no expert. For perhaps being carried away by one's theme is the same thing as to lack the discrimination to identify errors. For Ion, our paradigmatic non-expert, can comment on things only positively or not at all (535E).

But here is why this hypothesis seems incorrect. The objection simply misses its target. Socrates is not saying that one cannot be in an evaluative state of mind and none the less comment on things negatively. He is saying, and Ion is saying, merely that Ion is not. So he is not objecting to individuation through preferential action. He can be viewed as saying merely that an expert must conform to his third requirement in (i) while retaining an evaluative viewpoint. For an evaluative agent can seemingly comment on things negatively as well as positively. Such an agent can e.g. contradict or resist contact with a certain object or express mild approval; she need not simply be indifferent to it even if she does not absolutely affirm it. In chapter 2 and above in this chapter (3) we have actually seen Socrates represent evaluations as coming in degrees, so that a pot or horse can be somewhat or apparently fine though it is not properly, and a cook and a doctor can resemble the free without really being free. Hence, Ion need not be viewed as an example of preferential action in general. (It would indeed be uncharitable to attribute to Socrates the converse view, that criticism is to come from an indifferent perspective. *Of course* it is an interested one; *how* it is interested is the entire issue.)

In sum of 3.4., in the *Ion* Socrates praises and connects properties that are specific to the good in the *Lysis* though he does not explicitly discuss good.

3.5. Support from the *Hippias Minor*

In the *Hippias Minor* Socrates seems to say things about good which he was already found to say in the *Lysis*. I will now describe two points of agreement.

First, his topic is now the standard on which one man (human, agent) can be ranked above another (363A-B, 364B). Hippias says that better men are false, i.e. such as to mislead others on purpose (365B-C). But he means really to praise skill, or the ability to do what one wants when one wants it (366C). Socrates agrees with this (and indeed it is he who proposes the preceding definition of skill). Beyond this he wants in this dialogue merely to point out implications of this view. These he means to seem problematic, but it does not appear that he wants them to indicate that skill is not good. In this way, he seems to agree with the *Lysis* about good. For in both dialogues the good are self-sufficient in some way. They do what they want.[9]

Second, Socrates says that one is to relate freely to ends, and this is as in the *Lysis*. For he says that it is a matter of importance how one relates to ends, not just which ends one relates to. He says even that it is better to relate freely to negative external ends than non-freely to positive ones (372D-E).[10]

This is not quite to say, perhaps, that one should stand above external ends entirely, disparaging their importance, or that all that matters is one's relations to things. For the option remains that though free relations to negative things are better than non-free relations to positive things, free relations to positive ones rank higher still. If Socrates said this in the *Hippias Minor* then he would be even closer to the *Lysis'* view than he just was. But he does not seem ever quite to affirm or deny such a value in this dialogue. So he goes in a similar direction, only not as far.

3.6. Support from the *Cratylus*

Socrates' views in the *Cratylus* also seem to support the view of good that we found in the *Lysis*. But as in 3.4. and 3.5. the support does not extend to all points. So the shortcoming is only a limitation of scope and not, seemingly, any ambiguity or lack of explicitness. Before I list points of agreement let me note briefly what this dialogue discusses.

This dialogue's concern is with communication. But its aim is not to find commonalities specific to actual, historical cases of communication, so it does not aim at an analysis or explanation of natural language or any other symbolic system as it is, has been, or predictably will be. This is clear from its recurrent criticisms of various linguistic practices. Like other Socratic dialogues its concern is normative. Communication is here idealized about specifically for Socrates' educational purpose. He wants to identify patterns of a perfect sort of communication that is seldom if ever found in everyday life. What is it like?

In general, it is remarkably well suited for good processes as the *Lysis* seemed to view them in 3.1. and 3.2. For it involves the productivity of things alike to themselves by ends. Only now these products are thought of as ideal *symbols*. I will now convey this by listing three features of ideal communication as it is described in the *Cratylus*. (As before, no complete survey of the dialogue at issue is intended.)

First, symbols should be like the objects they are about (433D-E, 435C-D). This is as if one symbolized a horse by imitating one (423A), i.e. by having its properties. A symbol of Cratylus would perhaps be a perfect copy of him (432A), in which case the symbol and the object would be indistinguishable from each other.

The relation between symbol and object should, then, be something like correspondence. In contrast, if a system of symbols were consistent then this would not indicate that it should be relied on because it could be consistently mistaken (433D-E, 436B-E). Socrates seems here also to be implying that one could not analyze or translate one's way through to a correct view because consistency between languages, just like within any one of them, would not rule out error about external topics. One cannot be confident without further ado that customary views are correct. One needs foundations; consistency is not decisive.

This is not per se to discuss the issue whether e.g. yellow objects are natural to group together by using a single word whatever that word may be. Rather, the symbol should be especially fitted to its object. I.e., it is critical how one refers, not (at present) whether what one refers to is naturally distinct, e.g. of a natural kind. But why is it critical how one refers? What is Socrates after?

Second, the object of a symbol is an aim to which the symbol guides its perceiver (388A-C), so symbols are ethical tools, epistemologically and causally, in that they edify and that they (or their uses) have certain effects.

We can see based on this why a symbol should be like its object. If it were not, it would not per se direct one to that object. It would direct one to that object indirectly at most, namely by reference to other symbols. But if the guidance were thus indirect then a symbol system would be relied on, and then we would be back with coherence versus correspondence, and systematic error would again be a possibility.

Third, if S is a symbol for O, O produces S, for producers are like their products (393B-C, 394D). One's offspring will have one's own properties. Hence, the failure to produce a copy of oneself would simply be a failure to produce. Quantitatively, to the degree that one produces anything, it is copies of oneself that one produces.

What is so agreeable about these ideas from the *Lysis*' point of view is, as noted, that now aims are productive of things of their own kind.

The *Cratylus* does seem to disagree with the *Lysis* on some points also, however. It omits that the good should produce offspring not like themselves but better (though within the bounds of the same kind).[11] As lesser points, the *Cratylus* seems in fact to value changelessness (439D-E). It also says that good is, though abstract (389D-390A), compound (422A-B). In these ways, I admit that the *Cratylus* contradicts the *Lysis* (as it was interpreted above, in 3.1. and 3.2.). But we saw three supportive points also, so there seems to be some agreement.

3.7. The Irrelevance of the *Charmides*

It may seem that Socrates says things against the *Lysis'* (self-developmental) view of good in the *Charmides*. In this section (3.7.) I want to point out briefly why that is not so.

Here is one way one might think that he is opposed to the present view of good in this dialogue. He seems to question that anything can be intrinsically self-policed. For he says that in many instances objects of intentions are not those self-same intentions (166A-B, 167C-168A). His interlocutor points out, however, that this analogy is not conclusive, for perhaps "temperate" things are unlike the other things Socrates lists, not like them (165E-166A, 166B-C). Hence we should view Socrates' hypothesis as not entirely serious. It is but a hypothesis that runs into obstacles it does not overcome; it is not a part of his stable (or developing) position which consists of ideas he himself never contradicts.

A second objection Socrates can seem to offer against the possibility of self-sufficiency in the *Charmides* is that if x polices y then perhaps x needs to be greater than y in some sense (168B-D), e.g. so as to be capable of overpowering y. If x cannot overpower y, then perhaps x cannot control y. But then if x controls x then x is greater than x, impossibly. This may be what Socrates means at ibid. But this issue is irrelevant in that the good on our hypothesis do not overpower or control their objects. The good do not control what is worse (of lesser value or power) than themselves but rather they effect what is of more value than themselves. (They do not relate negatively or descriptively to anything due to teleological individuation. If something is teleologically individuated then it is identified by its end, not by its current or its past states. More specifically, a teleologically individuated thing *itself* measures only its own aim, not its current or past states.)

A more general reason to think that Socrates' views in the *Charmides* do not contradict the identification of good with self-sufficiency is that the topic of the *Charmides* is not good but right. It is right that relates positively to (all) things worse (not better) than itself. I will explain in chapter 5 and in section 6.3. in what ways this dialogue is about right. It discusses right quite like many other Socratic dialogues do. It is no objection at all to say that it discusses right in a different way than any dialogue discusses good. For Socrates himself stresses the difference between what we are calling right and good, or extrinsic and intrinsic relations and value. I will discuss this dichotomy many times in later chapters of this essay.

3.8. An Interpretive Objection

Socrates may adhere to a kind of "psychologism" in thinking that evaluative self-relations are involved in evaluative relations generally. This would be a descriptive claim. For at Lysis 205D-E Socrates says that Hippothales' praise of his lover is really praise of Hippothales himself. For in praising his lover as his lover in a reciprocal relation Hippothales indicates that this praiseworthy agent thinks him, Hippothales, praiseworthy in return. So someone he claims to be praiseworthy thinks him praiseworthy also—which would be praise from a high quarter (according to Hippothales).

This may be meant as a general psychological point about evaluation. For if we praise certain ends perhaps we praise ourselves as deserving their attainment. (Thus viewed, the point would not depend on reciprocity.)

If Socrates means to generalize in this sense then he is not *for* self-relations. They would now be a given. They may be implicit despite being a given, just as at 205E Hippothales does not at first see in what sense he is in an evaluative self-relation though he really is, as he acknowledges (ibid.). What Socrates would be for now would be a certain self-relations in particular, namely ones which satisfy intrinsically. (Which these would be was discussed in 3.2.)

The weakness of this psychological strategy would be that now self-relating is seen merely as inevitable. It would not be anything desirable. But if that were so then seemingly Socrates could not argue for it based on his tools, for his tools have seemed to be normative ones, consisting of evaluative thought-experiments. These do not say what everyone inevitably desires but what they ought to, when enlightened about their self-interest.

Things are different if Socrates means in this passage to say that Hippothales has *reason* to praise not only his end but also his relation to it. It would then not be something to which Hippothales is committed whether he wants to be that or not. But if Hippothales *should* want to praise his relation to his end then this should be because it would satisfy him as a self-interested agent. But why would this satisfy him? Well, he would be *happy*, i.e. self-sufficient, see 3.2., or at least happ*ier* than without it because now he would depend *less* on others and more on himself.

So it seems that in the name of charity we can view *Lysis* 205D-E as asserting not a psychologically inevitable self-relation but a normative and rationally desirable one. But if so, then the above objection would be false. For now we would take this passage to require a self-relation quite directly, not only as something implied by Socrates' view of happiness or his craft analogies in 3.2.

This passage would then need to be interpreted as follows. Hippothales "really" desires what he desires *when enlightened*, i.e. as a conclusion of a normative argument. This would not be a psychological thesis because now real desires would be normatively identified. The trouble with this is only that 205D-E seems to be phrased descriptively as about inevitable commitments and not as a piece of ethics, i.e. as saying what is worth desiring.

3.9. An Objection from Luck and Misfortune

It is x that should find (discover) y—though x does not plan this act in advance. But can x be responsible for something she has not planned for in advance? Is this not a matter of luck?

On the other hand, would it not be a misfortune to end up in a causal pattern from which one could not escape? If it compelled one to move in a certain way then would this not be an imprisonment?

In reply, one needs here to keep two senses of freedom well apart so that Socrates' position does not seem misled due to mere misunderstandings. On the one hand there is the freedom of the good and on the other that of the right. The good do not choose to become good independently of their situations. They are lucky to *become* good. But the process they undergo as good things is an intrinsically evolving one and it leaves nothing to luck. It feeds itself. It does not take any planning. There is no chanciness or leeway in it. When in it, one knows exactly what to do next and one can do it—and one does it. This does not sound like a lucky process. It sounds like a process in which precisely *nothing* is left to luck. One does everything relevant oneself. So seemingly one comes across and attains good partly by luck but a good process is not a lucky one.

But in chapter 6 we will find that coming across good is not *entirely* a matter of luck, for it presupposes doing right. The helpless need to open up before they can receive the appropriate kind of help. *They* must do that; it is up to them.

The alternative suspicion was that good causes are perhaps not too lucky but too *un*lucky to qualify as responsible ones. For what if one chanced to want to leap out of a good process? Could one do it or not? If not, would one not be *imprisoned* in it? Would the patterned process not form a kind of cage to which the events occurring in it are confined? In reply, one could not escape but nor would one want to. It would not even occur to one. This would not be due to manipulation but to the things one gets to want and the power one has to attain them. Better ends would actually be revealed before one's very eyes. In such a state, what reason could there possibly be to want to escape?

The possibility of escape is relevant in a different context. For goodness in the above sense is none the less the end to which Socrates thinks we should *strive* if my interpretation is correct. That striving—and the associated planning and reconsidering—is right. It is this striving that we can chose to do independently of our situation. We can always do otherwise—until we are good. But we do wish to become good (self-sufficient), one can insist, not to keep on bouncing from one unconvincing (or unattainable) aim to another, always hesitating or pretending and never exercising our wills properly.[12]

In these ways, it would not seem to be lucky or unlucky to continue in a good process after having (with some luck) arrived inside it. It would seem responsible, i.e. fitted for causal attributions.

3.10. Summary

In this chapter (3) we saw that Socrates says that good things produce other things which they rank above themselves (3.1.-3.2.). This criterion seemed at least possibly to be Socrates' best one by his own lights (3.3.). Similar ideas were found in other dialogues (3.4.-3.6.). In 3.7. we saw that Socrates is not opposed to this view of good in the *Charmides* and in 3.8.-3.9. that some objections to him are not as problematic as they may seem.

Notes

1. A different way to try to avoid the paradox would be by saying that it does not concern good. For one may say that if x is good at all—*intrinsically* valuable—then x is so independently of whether any non-x happens to think it is or not, or whether any non-x is satisfied by it, or whether any non-x relates to it in *any* way. For x is good intrinsically, not relationally to anything external to itself, or x is not good. For intrinsic value must reside in an object intrinsically.

The problem with this is that it flies in the face of Socrates' egoistic premises. For him it is not possible, logically, for anything to have intrinsic value without its satisfying agents. What is intrinsically valuable benefits them, and so they have reason to seek it. Socrates' very means of identifying good base on this assumption, so he continually asks whether x is satisfactory in one sense or another. This is so, I believe, even when he praises intrinsicness, for he then means to praise a *satisfying* kind of intrinsicness.

But of course some philosophers may oppose Socrates' egoistic assumptions. This possibility was briefly discussed in the beginning of chapter 1.

2. In fact, viewing things in terms of satisfaction or dissatisfaction may easily lead one to be caught inside the paradox of the will. For these things are formulated in terms of wanting (and having). But wanting (at least as it appears in the paradox) is a relation of *external dependency*. If I want to do x, or if I want to have y, then x or y will need to lie at some distance from me. If I could just do x, or have y, whenever I want to, then I would not need to waste time wanting to do x or wanting to have y: I would just do x, and have y. In this respect wanting is more like hoping than like doing anything oneself, such as building, speaking, looking, leaping, etc. It reflects a distance to an object, not an immediate contact.

Given this, one can notice that the paradox is phrased to describe not the activities of the independent or self-sufficient but rather the hopes of the *de*pendent, i.e. of those relating to what is beyond their own reach. So if wanting were necessary to satisfaction then the absence of independence or self-sufficiency, which solve the paradox, would be *implied*. Conversely, if we look at a list of free relations—namely the self-sufficient ones that solve the paradox—then wanting is not on our list. Accordingly, instead of exhibiting such relations as wanting or having we should exhibit others—the ones that allow us to avoid the paradox.

(Having as it is connected to wanting in the paradox needs no separate attention. For in that connection it stands for what was wanted before but which now is attained, or possessed, owned, etc., and though other kinds of having exist too, as having a pain, etc., they do not matter here.)

3. This problem is similar (not identical) to the paradox of inquiry in the *Euthydemus* (275D-278C) and the *Meno* (80D-E).

4. I wanted to avoid the repetitive alternative that x=y=z in value but not in content. On this alternative one would not advance after a certain point in the process. There would be variation only. This to me resembles the kind of "rat race" value that the paradox of the will should deny, for on this repetitive alternative one's actions do not lead one (after a certain point in the process) to be any better positioned than one was before performing them.

5. Marx seems to move in similar territory in his early essay "Money" when he says

(on pp. 193-194): (...) *love can only be exchanged for love, trust for trust, etc. If you wish to enjoy art you must be an artistically cultivated person; if you wish to influence other people you must be a person who really has a stimulating and encouraging effect upon others. Every one of your relations to man and to nature must be a* specific expression, corresponding to the object of your will, of your *real individual life. If you love without evoking love in return, i.e. if you are not able, by the* manifestation *of yourself as a loving person, to make yourself a* beloved person, *then your love is impotent and a misfortune.* (Cursives in original.) Marx opposes what he takes to be the tyrannical role of money and comes rather close to advocating the Socratic view of good. However, the match is not exact because Marx's values are not entirely self-relational.

6. The reader has much to make use of in speech acts, for apparently there are almost as many ways to be self-sufficient in Socrates' sense as there are to abstract in language. For one may typically reveal some salient property not only by telling the truth but also by promising, reminding, or even by joking or thanking, and if that is so, then each of these speech acts revises something, whether by discovering it or by creating or something else.

Not quite *every* speech act relates well to itself, and thanking is an example of this. If someone brings to your attention the thing she thanks you for, it is not worth anyone's time to call attention to the fact that she thanked you. That is obvious enough already. In a sense, thanking is this objective. It is little more than a way to bring a thing to someone's attention, namely that one noticed how she helped.

Still, this leaves one with many candidates because a lot of speech is not simply about noting things but about reshaping them for some purpose. For instance, one may promise to promise in a way that is less about forbidding something than promising is ordinarily (as in "I promise never to smoke again"), or one may remind someone of the way reminding was done before, e.g., with more respect than currently, with less immersion in the present. On the variety of speech acts in English, see Wierzbicka.

It does not appear to be a cause for worry if the speech acts overlap before or after the reforms, because each of them is after all to take care only of itself. No overall comparative viewpoint about speech acts seems necessary. For some overall viewpoints, see Vendler and Katz.

7. Does Socrates mean in the *Ion* or in the *Lysis* that experts or the good initiate causal chains in what is otherwise a causal vacuum or that they intervene in pre-existent chains? He does not seem to choose between these options in either dialogue. In the *Phaedo* we seem to find something like the former view, however, for in that dialogue apparently only ethical relations are causal (95A-100A), see chapter 7.

8. This may be to be to say that a failed attempt in a craft (or at independence, goodness) ranks above a non-attempt though the former receives negative treatment and the latter is ignored. If it is, then we have here an interesting piece of information about the intermediate-level objects that Socratic communication seemed in chapter 2 and above in this chapter (3) to presuppose. In chapter 2 such objects were fine pots and horses, and above in this chapter they were cooks and doctors. If they are to be viewed as failed attempts (at independence, goodness) which are to be treated negatively then this is something we have not heard before. (This is not news about good per se, however, or the good are not independent. For it is not up to them, qua independent, that appropriate intermediate-level objects are available at all. Communication about goodness, not goodness, presupposes intermediate-level objects.)

If the preceding impression is correct and a<b<c, then c receives a "Yes", b a "No", and a no reaction at all. Illustratively, c is loved, b *hated*, a ignored. On a different pattern, one would rather say "No" to a and ignore b, hence expressing mild approval or indifference for what has moderate value. This more graduated pattern is perhaps closer to common sense. It may in fact be Heraclitus', see 2.5.

In 3.5. below Socrates will suggest again that intermediate-level objects are (voluntary) attempts at something.

9. Actually, the *Hippias Minor* seems to say at 366C that they *can* do what they want, not that they necessarily do do it in fact. I ignore this nuance here.

10. This is presented as implying something troublesome, for it is contrary to a judicial point of view. For in court it is voluntary evils and not involuntary acts of any kind that are punished (370E). (If Karl did not do it, *Karl* is innocent—even if what happened was bad.)

Is Socrates opposed to this judicial norm? In my view, he seems to have something like a judicial norm based rather on right than on good, for only doing right is open to all; see chapter 6.

11. A few points fall into place if the offspring are better: first, there is a clear motive for producing them; second, the paradox of the will is avoided.

12. The tunnel problem (see 3.1.) does not leave us bumping around aimlessly for even though in a good process we lack security about its outcome (whether there will be *any* outcome, what it would or will be *exactly*) we still have stable direction because then we know in advance what *kind* of thing that next step would be (to qualify as belonging into the same process).

A deeper risk may be involved on a different side, however, for in starting down one tunnel we may err in not having started down a different one instead. This is so if there are several. Logically there can be several of them, for it is not inconsistent (unfree) of the free to say e.g. that sincerity about sincerity is not particularly sincere. Saying that would be only *insincere*. But that may not decide the issue for them if they face other tunnels (processes) to choose. For no tunnel will compel them *as opposed to another*, as each will compel only intrinsically (see 2.2. on exclusiveness). But though this pluralism is a logical possibility I think we should not worry about it too soon because perhaps we will rather have difficulties due to our finding too *few* candidate good things, not too many. Maybe we will not find *any*.

Chapter 4

RIGHT IN THE *EUTHYPHRO*

Chapters 1-3 discussed Socrates' criteria for good. In 4-6 our topic will be his criteria for *right*. Socrates sees good and right as different so his criteria for good do not pick out the same thing as his criteria for right. In other words, it would be an error to think of his definitions as all being about the same things. Some are about one thing, namely what I am calling "good," and some about another which I am calling "right."

How do I know that he has two different things to define? Could there not be one, three, or thirteen? The answer to this is not that he uses individual words consistently. Rather, the definitions themselves differ formally and deeply on some points but not on others. How do they differ? Roughly, some of the definitions requite intrinsic entities (i.e. intrinsic properties, relations, or whatever) and others require extrinsic ones. But the more exact difference between right and good will be explained only gradually in 4-6 as we proceed. Their appropriate relation is one of the topics of chapter 6.

The basic setting with right is the same as with good, however, for once again we need guidance as to how to recognize a universal (only this time it is right), and based on this knowledge of a universal we can come to identify its instances. For just like good, right is special. But like good, right is not pre-theoretically obvious. We are regularly misled about what right is and hence about what is right. Moreover, right is picked out by using criteria, and the criteria solve problems. So it is desirable to view right in some way versus others. I.e., it is not metaphysical reflections about reality that come first but practical (rational, self-interested) ones. For deliberative agents (not e.g. scientists with world-views) are to be persuaded by Socrates' arguments. They are Socrates' audience and it is their needs, however unconscious before the *elenchus* unfolds, that Socrates addresses.

What problems do Socrates' criteria of right solve? Only a single one which he describes in the *Apology*. I will be more elaborate on it in 6.1. but it needs now to be summarized so that Socrates' motive for saying what he says in chapters 4 and 5 is apparent to the reader. The problem is that if x is not good then x cannot know how to seek to become good. This is because to be able to identify good is to *be* good. It is impossible to know good and yet not to be good. This follows from what was said in chapters 2 and 3. But one ought to become good or one faces the problems discussed in chapters 1-3 (e.g. the "paradox of the will"). Socrates himself faces this problem (that he ought to become good but does not see how to do it) early in his career, he tells us in the *Apology*. He is aware that he is not wise, but his ignorance is so radical that he does not even know where to look for wisdom. So all that he knows is that his internal resources will not help him forward. Introspection will not do because the standard of good is intrinsic to the good and he is not good. His imaginative powers are hence too poor. He responds to this problem by opening up to everyone, indiscriminately, for clues about good. He is everyone's pupil, treating everyone as an ethical authority and as an independent thinker. He looks to young and old and rich and poor, etc. This response is *right*.

In this chapter (4) we focus on the *Euthyphro*. In this dialogue Socrates says that a standard of right will fit into any world, for it can be used to assess various candidates of right (4.1.). Good, by contrast, is found only in worlds which have no negative parts (see 1) or in which it is perfectly alone (2,3). Also unlike good, instances of right will be epistemically extrinsic, not intrinsic (4.2.). One can neither identify nor instantiate right intrinsically. (This is once again simultaneously a metaphysical and an epistemological point: right resides in an extrinsic relation of x to y (and x≠y), and right can be recognized in precisely that relation.) The *Charmides* advances similar ideas (4.3.).

4.1. Maximal

In the *Euthyphro* Socrates discusses piety, not right. But I will show gradually in this chapter (4) and in chapters 5 and 6 that he means hereby to discuss virtue generally and that his view of virtue can be seen as a conception of right. I will say that he discusses right already now so that this discussion remains simple.

At 6E Socrates asks Euthyphro for something to which he might look to compare candidate cases of piety thereby to decide conclusively whether they are pious things or not. But Socrates is now not after any example of piety, he says (6C-E). This is unlike what he required concerning good in chapter 2, for in the *Hippias Major* he inquired simultaneously into a standard and a perfect instance. But before inspecting the differences between right and good in 4.2., let us ask: (a) What must a standard be like to enable the needed work of measuring things other than itself? And: (b) Why must such measuring take place at all?

(a) We can see that Euthyphro's answer at 6E-7A (Jowett: "Piety, then, is that which is dear to the gods, and impiety is that which is not dear to them") is dissatisfactory because it has contradictory implications (because the gods happen to disagree amongst themselves: 7B, 7D-E). Hence it cannot "quickly end" differences by measuring (7C). So, we can draw, a standard must be simple and consistent so that it can be based on to resolve disputes, unambiguously and economically.

But we can be more precise than this, for the dialogue supplies us with more material. For at 8B Euthyphro protests that if the gods do not disagree about *everything*, then they will rule unambiguously about some instances, and so his answer is not entirely unfitting. I.e., he claims that his standard will do for present purposes, even if it is not eternally applicable. But Socrates replies that a standard must be unambiguous about *all possible* instances (6D), so it does not help Euthyphro's answer that the gods agree on some scores. I.e., if the standard does not work in all possible cases then it is not properly applicable to any.

One fault of Euthyphro's purported standard may, then, perhaps be put thus. It consists of properties x and y such that $x \neq y$ and some instance, A, has both x and y, B has neither, C has x and not y, and D y and not x. A and B receive unambiguous treatment but there is indecision as to whether C or D is right, in particular in contexts in which both C and D are options but in a mutually exclusive way. (For if we encountered C but not D, we would say yes to C due to x but no due to y. We would perhaps affirm C despite its imperfection in such a case. But if we came by both C and D and we had to choose either versus both, then saying yes to C would imply saying no to D, and vice versa. Here we would not avoid a contradiction. Because there is at least one such situation, Euthyphro's standard is faulty. It is faulty because it is complex.[1]) Socrates is saying that even though an actual instance which we happen to confront may be as A or B, the very possibility that C and/or D might be met implies that Euthyphro's purported standard is not an authoritative one.

Observe that this is not to say that this desired sort of consistency implies primitiveness. For a standard of right need not be lonely. It is instead to be paired with other things to measure those other things. Indeed, it is potentially to be used measure *any* thing other than itself. I will use the term "maximal" for this (a similar use is in Jubien pp. 139-140). x is not maximal if there is a world into which x cannot be fitted. So not only is our standard of right to be partless (as in the preceding paragraph), for it is also to be in a sense cosmopolitan. So perhaps Euthyphro's mistake is not only that his standard is too complex and hence potentially contradictory, but also that it will not be meaningful or relevant in many enough disputed cases. Its scope can be too narrow; and primitiveness does not imply width of scope. For perhaps the gods just do not say *anything* about some disputed issue, rather than being ambiguous about it. Maximalness, however, seems to imply non-complexity: if x is ambiguous between any two alternatives then x is not maximal, but if x is complex then seemingly x is ambiguous between some alternatives in the sense explained already (in this section, 4.1.). If so, we can take maximalness to go to the heart of the matter and non-complexity to be merely implied.

10A is an interpretive basis for the claim that Socrates wants a standard of right to measure things other than itself (i.e. to be applicable to more things than right ones, and hence to be *negatively* applicable in some sense).[2] For either one carries or is carried, sees or is seen, or loves or is loved, but not both at once.

Given that Socrates is after a *standard* of piety (see 6E-7C) it seems correct to interpret him as meaning which of these two things *justifies* which, being loved by gods and being holy. The point of the passage is to make Euthyphro choose between these two options; x is either a standard of piety (right) or a case of it, not both. He cannot have it both ways. But why not? I.e., what is it about piety or right that makes it unlike good, so that it cannot be at once a standard and a superlative instance? This is not explained in the *Euthyphro* but it will be in the *Apology* in chapter 6.

(b) Let us assume that any standard of right must be as described in (a). Still we can ask why a standard for right is needed at all. Why, in particular, cannot the cases we confront speak for themselves? What do we need rules for? Why would we, as it were, tie ourselves down voluntarily (by accepting our particular intuitions only if they conform to a maximal standard)? And why would the anti-social Thrasymachus or Callicles or their more recent analogues do so?

At 9E Socrates asks Euthyphro whether they should premise on mere assumptions or inspect the hypotheses they are considering themselves. The basic idea Socrates is expressing may be the one that already became familiar earlier in this essay: one needs to view in broad day light what it is that one is for or one cannot really be said to be for *it* in particular (see chapter 1). This time the clarity at issue would be different, for now the clear objects would be maximal not primitive.

But there would be a similar fault in this motive, for it could be insisted that now decision-making is being bound by something non-ethical. For maximalness is no more a directly ethical requirement than primitiveness or exclusiveness is. Evaluation could hence be seen now as being confined from without, not as being enabled from within. As noted, we need to wait until chapter 6 and the *Apology* to find a more plausible motive.

4.2. Different from Good

If we view right as Socrates requires in the *Euthyphro*, we are committed to viewing right or its standard as different from good in at least two respects. First, good is self-evident (see chapters 2-3), right not. For x is identified to be right by some non-x or other, not x itself. Second, good cannot exist in a world that contains its "contrary" (i.e., something negative, see 1.1.), but for our standard of right there is no such "contrary." It can, logically, exist in any world. (It can also concern things in negative worlds instead of simply not applying to them. Chapter 5 will expand on this.)

Further differences between good on the one hand and right and its standard on the other will emerge in 4 and 5 below.

4.3. Support from the *Charmides*

In the *Charmides*, Socrates says that to be temperate is at least to keep guard of oneself. For the temperate want to consume nothing in excess, so that such consumption will not interfere with their other or main project or projects. To this end, the temperate must be able to identify temperance (158E-159A). But also, they must relate their conception of temperance to multiple other things, even ones that do not accord with it, for this way they can police their impulses (159A-160D). The things policed and what polices them are now independent, just as the *Euthyphro* required of cases of piety.

Because these dialogues (*Euthyphro*, *Charmides*) say the same thing about different virtues, the things said about them are ones that hold not only for particular virtues but for virtue more generally. Indeed, if the same criterion (namely maximalness) is used to identify both virtues, temperance and piety, precisely the same things will be identified. Hence, temperance and piety will not merely resemble each other or overlap, they will be one and the same thing, only differently termed. The plurality of terms or descriptions would then hide the deeper and unified reality that is exposed by using a criterion. The thesis that for Socrates only one thing is virtuous or right will receive more support below.

4.4. Summary

In this chapter (4) we saw that in the *Euthyphro* Socrates demands a standard for right that is independent of cases of right and which standard is also maximal (i.e., ambiguous about nothing outside itself) (4.1.). In the *Charmides* he required the same (4.3.). This criterion of right makes right rather different from good (4.2.). But we were also left puzzled about why Socrates propagates this criterion for any kind of value (right) at all, i.e. in what way this criterion is not merely conceptual but ethical (4.1.).

Notes

1. Why then could one not simply rate x above or below y and retain a complex standard? Perhaps one would miss out on economy, somewhat. But a second downside in it could be that the ranking of x above y would again need a standard.

2. Also see 10B-11B.

Chapter 5

RIGHT IN THE *CHARMIDES*

In the *Charmides*, discussed in this chapter (5), Socrates says that the right need to interact with all possible others in a single positive way. More pointedly, x is right only if x is valuable in any world which contains any non-x. In other words, it must be what I will call an "extrinsic end": it has value qua related to all possible things outside itself (so it is extrinsic), but its value is not per se instrumental (so it is an end). This is the criterion the early Plato invokes most often (for anything), I believe, but the clearest passage that expresses it is in the *Charmides* (5.1.). Chapter 6 will relate this criterion to the one in 4 and expose Socrates' motive for propagating it.

This criterion is distinct from the criterion of exclusiveness (see chapter 1) in two ways. A *world* w which contains x and some non-x (y) need not have positive value for x to be right. It is *x* that must be positive *in* w, alongside or despite y. x need not buy y out, as it were, but it did in chapter 1. Second, Socrates often tests whether x is right by considering worlds in which y is *negative*. The testing in 1 always involved only *indifferent* y's. Hence, even though good and right both have value qua relational objects, the relations they have value in are different. (5.2.)

I will cite the *Republic,* book 1, and the *Laches* as supportive of the criterion of the relevant *Charmides* passage (5.3., 5.4.).

This criterion faces two potential problems. First, the criteria in chapters 4 and 5 can seem mutually independent from each other. Does Socrates think that these criteria pick out different objects, perhaps different kinds of value? Or is he after all himself offering a non-maximal, for a complex, standard for right (contrary to the *Euthyphro*, see chapter 4)? No, for in the *Apology* he will explain in what way these criteria are not mutually inconsistent but indeed to be understood as identical to each other (see chapter 6).

Second, it may seem that if but one thing is an extrinsic end then one must as it were live in a straight-jacket (5.5.). For apparently one will then always relate to other things in precisely the same way. That does not seem suitable, as different situations appear to require different responses. Moreover, it seems contrary to Socrates' cherished idea that one should grasp ethical meanings versus parroting them without creativity or responsiveness to stimuli. (He wants agents to justify their positions themselves and in relation to diverse criticisms, not merely to cite some authority or quote.) For if right is always the same then apparently its instantiations will be mere repetitions of each other. But given that right is a relation to all kinds of thing, it is open to Socrates to say that right actually resides in a single kind of thing that is particularly mobile and responsive, i.e. chameleon-like not parrot-like, and this too he will say in chapter 6.

5.1. An Extrinsic End

At 159A-160B Socrates says that Charmides is to determine whether x is temperate by noting whether x has *value*. x is to be "good," "noble," i.e. praiseworthy. But more exactly x is to have value (again as presently imagined) in all kinds of different circumstances, e.g. when boxing as when being taught. E.g. calm quietness is not temperate because it would not be valuable—says one's evaluative imagination—in all kinds of different context. It would have value at most in some. In other words, x is to be an extrinsic end. For it is to have value in whichever and not only some chosen context; and it need not have value in isolation; and also it is not indicated that it has value as a means. But let us go through these points more slowly.

Given that x is to have value in whichever context external to itself, x need not have value in isolation. That is not the type of value intended in the above passage. It would not be referred to as "temperate" and it would not be praised and commended in the sense that things referred to by that term should be. Rather, x's value is extrinsically relational: x when paired with any non-x must have value.

But notice also that though in the above passage value is relational, there is none the less no hint that it is merely instrumental to something else. Rather, if x is "temperate," and hence extrinsically an end, then x is praiseworthy due to its relation to other things simpliciter—not due to what will happen after, and not due to anything else extrinsic to the relation between x and the non-x at issue. It will be clear in chapter 6 that Socrates wants virtue or right to have instrumental value also. But that is not the only type of value it is to have. This we have learned from the above passage. In it temperance is identified evaluatively, as an end, and not due to any finding that it is effective in an instrumental role.

Now is the appropriate moment to justify my use of "right" for what Socrates intends.

In modern ethical theory it is common to distinguish between deontological or right-based and consequentialistic or good-based positions. It is the former kind that Socrates' view now belongs.

Right is usually seen as a valuable way of relating to something beyond oneself. Being relational to something external, right is not intrinsic. Right is, one may say, a way to approach a circumstance. Deontologists do not assign importance to the empirical consequences of such a relation. So their attitude is that one should do (or be) x no matter what the consequences of doing x will be. x is to be done not for the sake of an external reward. But also it is not to be done for its own sake (i.e. for itself qua isolated from every non-x) but for the sake of its extrinsic relation.

As an example, the deontologist Kant views e.g. truth-telling as right (though right is not Kant's usual term; he uses *gut* (good)). Telling the truth may not pay off. It may have terrible consequences. People may suffer, for example. But it none the less is something one should do. For its reward is not in its consequences. But still it is not intrinsic either, for telling the truth involves a party other than the person telling the truth (and also something other than the truth told), namely someone to whom the truth is revealed. Without an (intended) extrinsic relation, doing right is impossible. (Not so being good, recall.)

Besides Kant, another prominent deontologist in modern ethical theory is Ross. For him, there are various "*prima facie* duties," e.g. to keep one's promises. These are duties not because they pay off in rewarding consequences, but because of the way they relate to things outside themselves. Unlike Kantian duties, Ross's are *prima facie*, not "categorical," so they hold only "everything else being equal." One duty may override another. Whether it does depends on the circumstances. So Rossian duties are not only non-absolute: they are also responsive to, conditional on, some contexts versus others. By contrast, Kantian duties hold in all contexts.

Socrates' most frequent test for whether x is virtuous is whether x is a relational end, and this test does not involve the contemplation of x's consequences, and yet it involves the placing of value in an extrinsic relation. Hence, Socrates' criterion for virtue reveals that by "virtue" (*arête*) he means what moderns would mean by "right" (though that is not all he means by "virtue," see chapters 4 and 6). This justifies my use of the latter term in this essay.[1]

The *Charmides* does not explain why anyone ever must be temperate, however. I.e. it does not say why we should not seek some other type of value in its stead. For example, we might want to be particularists, or simply not to philosophize at all. Why must we go Socrates' way? In this dialogue he seems not to say. Nor does he appear to say in it how its criterion relates to that discussed in chapter 4. Chapter 6 will return to both points.

5.2. Relations to Criteria Presented Earlier

This criterion is differs from the one in chapter 1 in two ways. First, if x is a relational end, then x+y>0 even when y<0. (This is so in *Republic* 1 (5.3.) and *Laches* (5.4.), not the *Charmides* (5.1.). It suffices, however, that only some of the counterfactual contexts are negative, for x is to be identified as right in relation to *any* y, so some y's may be indifferent (or even positive, for good, see 6).) But if x is exclusive, then x+y>0 such that y=0 (see 1.1.). So right and good are identified based on different considerations, not the same ones. For doing right involves doing well in negative worlds, but being good does not. In other words, being good is not a matter of facing up to evils. But doing right, or being virtuous, e.g. courageous or temperate, is: one must face up to danger or fear or temptation, and not necessarily so as to annihilate it, but rather so as to have value despite the negative facts. In other words, the set of relations relevant to right is broader than such a relevant set is for good.

Second, if x is a relational end, then x+y>0 means that x has value despite the actuality of y. But if x is exclusive, then x+y>0 means that the sum of x and y is positive.[2] In other words, good makes[3] valuable what it relates to whereas right does not. For to do right is to relate to evils in such a way as not necessarily to cause those evils to no longer be evils. Right has value despite and alongside evils, one might say.

5.3. Support from *Republic* 1

At *Republic* 1 331E-332B Socrates interrogates Polemarchus about the virtue of justice. If Polemarchus' first definition (that repaying a debt is just; 331E) were correct, then justice would have negative value in some contexts, Socrates says (when a potentially dangerous item is returned to someone who is not in her right mind, 331E-332A); but justice has negative value in no contexts whatsoever, so the first definition is false. This is how Socrates argues in this passage. The premise that justice has value in every external context is his implicit requirement and it states that justice is an extrinsic end.

By implication, Socrates requires evaluative thought (i.e., thought about ends) of Polemarchus. If Polemarchus does not say what is worth desiring, he is simply not discussing justice (or virtue or right). Observe also that the counterinstance that Socrates presents (returning arms to someone not in his right mind) is quite hyperbolical. (Beyond this it is also a negative one, as noted in 5.2.) It works as a counterinstance not because it presents a scenario that Polemarchus now confronts or is likely to confront but because it is imaginable. So once again it is not actual or likely contexts but possible ones that are relevant when virtue or right is defined. As always, Socrates' test consists of an evaluative thought experiment.

To this background, the criterion for justice in the *Republic* (book 1) is exactly the same as the criterion for temperance in the *Charmides*. If the criterion is necessary and sufficient, it will pick out the same range of objects, so "justice" and "temperance" will be different words for the same thing.

But we cannot quite conclude from this that monism about virtue is correct because being an extrinsic end is not sufficient for virtue to Socrates (for maximalness is necessary also, see chapter 4) The thesis that there is only one Socratic virtue can be shown to be correct only once his complete conception of it is available in chapter 6.

5.4. Support from the *Laches*

At *Laches* 192C Socrates says that x cannot be courageous unless x is good and noble versus evil and hurtful, so courage is identified by evaluative means. But it is again thought experiments and not empirical tests that decide about values. More exactly the thought experiments consist of asking whether x has negative value in *any circumstances*, e.g. also when it is paired with pleasure or pain (192B) or foolishness (192D). Hence Socrates obviously views courage not only as imaginatively and evaluatively selected but as a particular way to relate to several different things external to oneself which have negative value. So he is once again using this same pattern to decide, with his interlocutor, whether x is virtuous or right. This time, if x is an extrinsic end, x is "courageous." But the criterion of identification is the same, so the situation is just the same as in the preceding section. Virtue or right in general seems to be intended.

But admittedly Socrates does not say in the above passage that courage or virtue should be identified relationally to *any possible* context, so this passage contains only some not all elements of his criterion that x is right only if x is an extrinsic end. Only a few contexts are mentioned. In this way, Socrates is more explicit in the *Charmides* and *Republic* 1 than in the *Laches*.

5.5. An Objection from Context-Sensitivity

In requiring that if x is right then x is a relational end, Socrates means to require, among other things, that only one thing be viewed as a relational end, see 5.1. above. He means to rule out the possibility that x has value in some contexts but not in others. But this is to say that there is only one valuable way to relate to things external to oneself, which is absurd, at least on two accounts. First, different circumstances seem to call for different approaches. For instance, one ought not to behave at a funeral as at a school, but both involve relations to negative things, namely death and ignorance respectively. Second, if Socrates believes it important that values be selected in full awareness, then adhering to the same x as right always would seem to make routine of doing right, and such routine may make of doing right a matter of unconscious habit, which is something he seems regularly to oppose (especially as "gadfly" in the Apology, see chapter 6).

In 6 we will see that though only one thing is right for Socrates, that one thing is a kind of responsiveness to situations, so the above objection falsely assumes that (a specific type of) sensitivity cannot be constant. To illustrate this with a metaphor, that only one thing is valuable in relation to things other than itself does not imply associations with parrot- or robot-like attitudes or actions, for the single thing that is meant can be precisely a kind of mobility and flexibility, just as a chameleon remains a single animal and in a sense consistent in its reactions and initiatives even though, or precisely because, the colours it manages to turn into are so varied (depending on where it happens to find itself).

5.6. Summary

In this chapter (5) we saw that in various dialogues Socrates requires that to be right, x must be an extrinsic end (5.1., 5.3., 5.4.). The differences to 2 were pointed out in 5.2. But some problems with this criterion were discovered also: it seemed unethical (5.5.) and its need and relation to maximalness were left unexplained (as noted in the introduction to this chapter, 5).

Notes

1. What, again, was the advantage of using "right" instead of "virtue" (or "virtuous")? As noted in the Introduction (0), complex associations seem to connect with the latter term but not with the former one. I.e., we can define right much more easily than virtue. But if we allow for complex associations then we will fail by Socrates' own lights, for he requires a simple and general view. Also, it seems so to happen that Socrates' own view is just as simple as he demands, so we do not appear to need any complex terms or associations to interpret what he means.

2. Obviously, "+" is now being used in two different ways, and it may obscure the situation that it is. But to use two different operators and to explain how they differ would have taken at least as long as to describe the difference as above. As before, my "technical" expressions are merely illustrative, not any kind of shorthand.

3. The "making" relation was analytic in chapter 1, evaluative in chapter 2, and productive-progressive in chapter 3.

Chapter 6

RIGHT IN THE *APOLOGY*

In the *Apology* Socrates finally explains his view of right. This is no longer merely a criterion of right but a substantial conception of it. This satisfies the criteria for it that were described in chapters 4 and 5. In this dialogue Socrates also implies how the criteria in chapters 4 and 5 relate to each other and invokes a problem in response to which agents have reason to do right in his sense.

As I explain in 6.1., in this dialogue he says that all should live the kind of examined life that he has lived. One lives this kind of life by seeking to learn from others about good. I.e., one seeks to be corrected from without about ends.[1] So right is a means to good.

In this same section (6.1.) I also clarify in what way this conception of right avoids a normative problem. The problem is that if you are not good then, by the criteria in chapters 2 and 3, you cannot identify good either. This is because good is epistemologically intrinsic (self-evident): to know good is to be good. If you knew what good is you would *be* good. If you are not, you do not. But your self-interest none the less lies in becoming good (or else you face the problems described in chapters 1-3, e.g. the "paradox of the will"). The problem that then faces you is that you cannot know how to seek what is in your self-interest. You see only that you cannot help yourself. This is Socrates' own situation early in his philosophical career as he documents it in the *Apology*. His response is to question others about wisdom (normative self-knowledge; good). He questions all others indiscriminately because he cannot say in advance who is wise. So the extroverted and instrumental view of right is a response to the problem that the non-good cannot know how to seek what they ought to seek.[2]

In 6.2. I turn to the relation of the examined life to the criteria in chapters 4 and 5. Cross-questioning is what all should do with others, Socrates says in the *Apology*, so he implies that this way of relating to others is an extrinsic end (compare chapter 5). But to relate in this way to another is not only to place one's standard of good outside oneself but also to take as right only what is logically unconnected to one's actually deciding to do right, so this same activity satisfies the criterion described in chapter 4. There will be some nuances to this relation to the criterion in 4, however.

In 6.2. I will also address the question how Socrates can claim to be both a consequentialist and deontologist about right. For he says, as above, that right is a means to good (in 6.1.), but also that right is an extrinsic end (in 6.2.). I will suggest that right is a necessary but not a sufficient cause of (the attainment of) good. Hence doing right is an unconditional duty for the non-good and also instrumental to good.

Various dialogues echo the *Apology*'s ideas (6.3.-6.6.), so these are not isolated ones in the early dialogues of Plato. In 6.7.-6.8. I consider objections to the *Apology*'s view of right and argue that they are not lethal to it.

6.1. Inquiry

Let us first summarize Socrates' problem about right. It arises in relation to his criteria of good as these were presented in chapters 2 and 3 above. These criteria say that only the good can identify good. For to identify it is to be it. (Criteria of good are accessible to the not-good also, but the criteria do not lead one directly to attain good. Grasping a criterion is one thing, its successful application another.) But if only the good can identify good and all have reason to seek to be good, then the non-good need to seek to become good without knowing what they are seeking. They are necessarily in the dark. This is the problem. It is a problem that faces all non-good agents. The problem is, to phrase it one more time, that precisely because they are not good the non-good cannot help themselves in becoming good.

This is Socrates' own situation earlier on in his philosophical career (*Apology* 21A-C). He is so ignorant that he does not know even in what sense anyone is wise (good). He responds to this problem by cross-examining others. Perhaps they are wise. At least he himself is not. He is not entitled to discriminate between them in advance of learning more about good. In fact, he cannot discriminate at all until he is good, or the criteria in chapters 2 and 3 are not criteria of good. He must welcome instruction from all. But this is what he does (30A).

In what way is social inquiry into good a response to the above problem? Obviously, social inquiry does not *guarantee* the attainment of good because one can inquire socially without happening to come by anyone good. So it is not a sufficient cause. But if not sufficient, it does seem necessary. For if it has already been found that one cannot produce x alone then seemingly it follows that *if* one is to produce x then only with the help of some non-x (if at all). It is then a further step to actually inquire for help.

Is it clear that Socrates means the above things? The *Apology* is easy to view as Socrates' account of his own characteristic activities and purposes. But it is clearly more than this: he intends to be exemplary, and he says so. Life is not worth living in any other way than his (20D-E, 21B-22E, 29D-30B, 30D-31A). He chastises his fellow Athenians for holding a contrary opinion (ibid.). In other words, they should be ashamed to rank e.g. money and honour above wisdom and truth (29D-E). Socrates' cross-examining does not always feature him in the questioning role and others in the role of answerer, for the converse is welcome to him also (33A-B). Persons from all walks of life, e.g. rich and poor, young and old (30A), but perhaps especially the unesteemed (22A), are welcome to take up either role in relation to Socrates. So this is the attitude all should have in relation to others. So not only does Socrates live an examined life by cross-examining others but he also wishes others to do the same. And what can be attained by living this life? Is it its own end? What can be attained is the best humanly attainable thing which Socrates claims uniquely to have attained; I speculated about what this may be in 3.8. above.

Here are some further and more detailed observations of Socrates' conception of right based on the *Apology* and some other dialogues.

Socrates clearly means that seeking instruction from others should be the main daily activity of all (non-good) agents. That is, it should take up much of the time and energy. Presumably he does not mean that agents should not eat or sleep. But much time and energy is according to him currently devoted to other things that should be sacrificed for the sake of doing right, and of these he mentioned the pursuits of money and honour.

Seeking to be corrected does now not mean submission to others. One's teacher owes one a clear account of good. In so far as she cannot provide this, she cannot count as a teacher and must herself become a pupil. There is, then, never a need to blindly take over her ideas. Teachers are accountable to students. But on the other hand, the teachers need not seek to please the students either. Public transparency and brevity can be required as general norms, both ways. This we see from virtually every early Platonic dialogue.

A student of good must be prepared to assess the oddest-seeming hypotheses, just as no hypothesis is too strange for Socrates to study it (provided it has purported ethical relevance) and no agent is rejected from intercourse (due to age, wealth, etc.)[3]. (On the other hand, presumably no hypothesis can be left to seem excessively odd for long, for authority presupposes transparency.[4])

Doing right cannot presuppose awareness of Socrates' criteria for good (in chapters 1-3) or right (chapters 4-5) or he cannot require agents to do right independently of their station. But he does seem to require that. He demands clear, brief, co-operative dialogue even from such untheoretical or anti-theoretical characters as Ion, Hippias, Thrasymachus, and Callicles. The obligation to try to improve oneself by seeking to be taught seems to be omnipresent to him. It is not something that one has a duty to only after attaining a certain educational level. But if this is so then what Socrates predicates right of must actually be at least somewhat familiar to agents from everyday life. It can be something that they occasionally practice but merely do not practice enough or in a pure enough way. At any rate it must be within their reach. But welcoming extrinsic correction about a variety of matters does seem to be an aspect of socialization (especially in childhood), so this would not be an absurd assumption among social beings.

6.2. Relations to the Criteria in 4-5

Seeking instruction from all others is something Socrates was just seen to prescribe to others as a general norm. They should live the examined life just as he does. It is the relation they should take to others in general. In this way, it looks like Socrates means hereby to describe in a substantial way what is right by the criterion in chapter 5. For now the examined life appears as an extrinsic end.

But the same thing appears also for him to satisfy the criterion in 4, in roughly the following sense. To live the examined life is to rely on an external standard. For those living the examined life place their standard outside their own bounds, namely in their relation to what lies without. They do not view themselves as authoritative but rather seek those who are. Because they welcome external correction they can be said to satisfy the criterion in chapter 4.

But this is a little imprecise on a few scores so let us go through a few questions. First, there is the point that in chapter 4 one qualified as right only on an external standard but now the right seek to relate to the *good*. They do not necessarily attain that external relation (see 6.1.), however, so that external relation cannot qualify them as right. Moreover, a relation to the good could not justify them as right because the standard of anyone good is not maximal (it does not relate to everything else) but a standard of right was in chapter 4. So what now is that external standard of right? For it is not anyone's sought after relation to good. In reply, we need to picture there being three orders of value. On the third there is a kind of conscience, which as a Socratic one tells one always to inquire of others into good (unless one is good already). This is the standard of right. On the second order there are our responses to that conscience: we either obey it or we do not, and accordingly we do right or wrong. On the first order we have our actual first-order conceptions of good. If we accept these and they are not good then we do not obey our consciences and do wrong. This, at least, seems like one coherent way to picture Socrates' meaning.[5]

A second problem is that it is not obvious in what way a standard of right, on the hypothesis of the preceding paragraph a conscience, can be maximal. I.e., how does the conscience spoken of in the preceding paragraph say in a determinate way for every possible case that it is either right or wrong? In reply, the conscience must always tell one to do the same exact thing, namely to take distance from one's first order view and to open up to what may always be better. If this sounds like a complex relation (and hence like a non-maximal one), then one charitable option is to say that probably Socrates views not the distance-taking per se as maximal but rather the (sincere) preparedness to believe what one is about to confront. It is at least arguable that this kind of a preparedness is in every case either present or not and that there are no ambiguous cases. For one's heart is in it or it is not, so to speak, and half-hearted efforts are not ambiguous cases but wrong acts. At least, this seems like one way to indicate that right is maximal.[6]

In the above ways we can view Socrates as providing more than criteria of right. Chapters 4 and 5 presented his criteria and now we have said in what ways he actually says what right is also.[7]

But if Socratic cross-examination (or, really, the effort to partake in it) satisfies the criterion in chapter 5 and it is also a means to good as in 6.1. then seemingly it is simultaneously both a deontological and a consequentialistic notion. But these two doctrines are commonly viewed as contrary to each other, for perhaps one needs to choose between thinking that (intrinsic) ends justify means and that (intrinsic) ends do not matter. Yet we do have interpretive backing for the thesis that Socrates attempts to embrace both doctrines at once. For we already noted that living the examined life should bring one the highest reward humanly possible (6.1.). Here he speaks as a consequentialist. But he also professes deontological ideas in the same dialogue: in deciding whether to live one way or another one is not to think about whether it pays off (with e.g. death or survival, 28B-D) but whether it has value per se or not, and yet right action consisted of relating to others so it is not intrinsic qua bearer of value. He also said in 6.1. that he wants to apply his norm to any possible situation and that he will not stop doing so as long as he lives. The outcome of the process, and hence whether the process turns out to be rewarding or not, will not stop him from following the procedure (29D, 30B). What entitles Socrates to speak both as an opportunistic instrumentalist and yet also as a principled ethician? We can speculate that doing right is a necessary but an insufficient cause of (the attainment of) good. If so, doing right is mandatory to all who are not good. It would be an inevitable means without which one could not advance one's self-interest.

But why would doing right be a necessary cause of becoming good? One needs to reflect that no other alternative but sincere extroversion is within the *intrinsic* powers of the non-good. They cannot e.g. count on the chance that the good will come to them or that a miracle will occur out of the blue that will reveal to them how to become good. Or at least they cannot do so without opening up socially. These options are beyond their control except for the move to extroversion. What is within their control is the move to inquire of others. If the others happen not to be there then this our candidates for right cannot help. But they can make the effort.[8] This should be the only way for the non-good themselves to react to their helpless state while basing on their intrinsic powers. If you will, doing right is the only non-helpless alternative open to the otherwise helpless. It is the only power every agent necessarily has (but only as an option that is conditional on a choice). Again, this is meant hypothetically as a way to see plausibility in Socrates' views.

Deontologists might protest that it is not right in a moral sense of the term to seek one's self-interest in this way any more than it is in others. But observe that to (attempt to) cross-examine others is in a sense to respect (and perhaps even to seek to enhance) others' free thought. For one will ask, and directly, and with a preparedness to hear very significant news. This seems like a very favourable way to treat another. Also, all possible others are at issue. E.g. the uneducated or foreigners are not to be biased against. For the right seek to make of any stranger their teacher.

Despite this, some deontologists would probably not be convinced, for the motive for doing right now remains self-interested. Perhaps many Christians or Kantians would deny that Socrates addresses real morality at all. For to Socrates the positive treatment of others is not antithetical to one's self-interest but intertwined with it. But to many non-Christians and non-Kantians, this same feature should appear as an advantage and not as a disadvantage in his position, for if he is correct then it would arguably be contrary to one's enlightened self-interest to be immoral. The self-interested could then potentially be converted to morality by means of argument.

6.3. Support from the *Charmides*

At *Charmides* 159A Socrates says that Charmides cannot be temperate without seeing what temperance is. He cannot be temperate accidentally, or without being aware of his being temperate. In other words, the only way to be temperate is by being so in a way that makes the content and justification of one's state or action obvious. There needs to be some fixed point (for whatever reason).

Socially, Charmides needs to intend Socrates to acknowledge that he is temperate or he is not temperate. This is because Charmides knows Greek so if he is himself aware of the nature of temperance then, Socrates says, he can probably tell Socrates what it is (ibid.). Hence temperance must consist at least in being able to attempt to do something publicly, at least among speakers of the same language. This can leave us with the impression that being temperate is necessarily to participate in cross-examination. If this is so, temperance seems similar to right as it is presented in the *Apology*.

However, it is not quite exactly so. For, first, admittedly the *Charmides* is not quite explicit that Charmides qualifies as temperate if he only *tries* to converse with Socrates in the appropriate way. Second, Socrates does not actually say that Charmides is temperate *in* making such an attempt. So this dialogue's agreement with the view of right that has been pictured earlier in this chapter (6) is only rough.

6.4. Support from the *Gorgias*

In the *Gorgias* Socrates repeatedly views being refuted by another as an act having positive value. It is something he strives for and the striving for which he propagates to others. He says that he is treated *well* if he is refuted (470C). Indeed, perhaps the best expression of the effort to do right in the Socratic sense is contained in this dialogue: to sincerely say to another, "Refute me!" (467B), or to state as a general norm, "refute and be refuted" (462A). So in the *Gorgias* social corrigibility is viewed as an extrinsic end, as it was above in the *Apology*.

But the *Gorgias* contains some nuances involved with this value that serve as more than supportive of the *Apology*. They actually make Socrates' view of right understandable in ways that the *Apology* does not discuss.

In the *Gorgias* Socrates seeks to bring to shame (494D) characters who are boastful and certain that they have ethical authority but who none the less have difficulty putting their views precisely or defensibly: Polus and Callicles. The way Socrates attempts to bring them to this negative state is by showing to them that they are not good, and hence that their self-importance has been unfounded. They have claimed to be something they are not, for they have claimed to be better than they are. Fundamentally, shame is the appropriate feeling to characters who lie about themselves in a sense relevant to good. This, then, appears to be one thing that Socrates means to chastise about Athenian lifestyles in the *Apology*. I.e., if attempted social inquiry into good is right, unfounded self-satisfaction (boastfulness at worst) is wrong.

It is important here that Polus and Callicles fail by their *own* lights. In other words, in Socrates' court it is the criminals themselves that need to be convinced of their guilt. This fits well with Socrates' views that to punish a criminal really should be to educate her about herself, for self-knowledge is the aim (*Apology* 28E-29A, 30B, 39D).[9]

Observe also that this moment of shame is achieved, or at least sought, by entirely fair means, for Polus and Callicles are given a full chance to show what they know. This is not to say that they are allowed to speak at great length or in any manner they may choose, but rather that they must explain themselves briefly and understandably. (I.e., a part of receiving a fair hearing is for Socrates that one's explanations are questioned. Even if what an interlocutor says is self-evident, that said thing must conform to certain criteria, so the said thing per se is not necessarily an authority as to whether it is self-evident or not.[10]) Because Polus and Callicles are treated fairly, they cannot themselves fairly protest that they have been mistreated or misrepresented. This should make their pain worse, for now they were treated well and they responded badly by boasting of knowledge which they lack. Their animosity was unprovoked. This should suggest even to them that the cause of their shame really was self-originated. But of course Socrates is quite open about his own and superior ways, so he is not locking them into their shameful state. Rather, due to the (publicly accessible, plausible, and essentially sympathetic) way that he inflicts self-knowledge onto them, he also simultaneously shows them a way to change.[11]

In these ways, the *Gorgias* seems to support the *Apology*'s view of right and also to explain a little more broadly why cross-examination might be viewed as a tribunal of social justice.

6.5. Support from the *Laches*

In the *Laches*, Socrates says that the virtue of courage is based on or identical with knowledge about good and bad (see 194E-195A, 195E-196A; in these passages his interlocutors express the relevant points, but the contexts make clear that these ideas are the ones Socrates has been driving at all along by suggesting them through the particular criticisms he has made of hypotheses that preceded them). This is to say that virtue is cognitive and directed at good, which is a view similar to the *Apology*'s on right. But even if Socrates means in the *Laches* that courage is identical to knowledge about good he would not thereby say that right is identical to the social study of good, for (i) courage may not be identical to right and (ii) knowledge may be non-identical to any kind of a social study.

(i) In 5.4. we saw that Socrates views courage as an "extrinsic end." But he views several other "virtues" as extrinsic ends also, see chapter 5. This may not per se indicate that the virtues are identical to each other for perhaps they form a complex extrinsic end jointly but without being identical to each other. But in chapter 4 we saw that at least the *Euthyphro* and a little more ambiguously in the *Charmides* views cases of virtue as justified on a maximal and external standard, and in 4.1. it was noted that such a standard does not seem to admit of complexity. Hence qua justified every virtuous act should be the same, so e.g. a case of courage should be identical a case of temperance (qua justified). In these ways, it seems that Socrates maintains that "courage" is but one of several alternative terms for a single property right.

But this is not to say that he maintains that in the *Laches*. For all we know he may suddenly take a different view of courage or virtue in this dialogue. For the *Laches* does not require a maximal and external standard for right acts.

(ii) One might argue that courage in the *Laches* is for Socrates a matter of knowledge about good and bad as attained, not as strived for, socially or otherwise. But at 194A he does say that striving for knowledge is at least one courageous thing. This leaves open the possibility that there are cases of courage which do not consist of the same striving, however, so we are not entitled to conclude that this striving is identical to courage in this dialogue.

So the *Laches* gives us only incomplete support of the *Apology*'s view of right but it is roughly supportive of it.

6.6. Support from the *Lysis*

In discussing the *Lysis* in chapter 3, I focused on what Socrates says about good in that dialogue. But another main theme in it is the nature of any rational agent who appreciates good but does not have that property. She is defined in part through the relation that is called for between her and good. Socrates says that such a relation necessarily involves activity on the part of the non-good agent, not of the good, for the good are self-sufficient and hence they are not in need of anything beyond themselves (215A-C). But a non-good agent has an interest in getting into contact with good. For contacts between the non-good and the good (or good) will benefit only the non-good, not the good. Hence, we can draw, every non-good agent must herself be aware that she must become active; otherwise she will never come into contact with the good (deliberately, at least). Moreover, like in other dialogues Socrates views the instrumental relation as an educational one in the *Lysis*, so the relevant contacts sought by the non-good with the good would be socially instructive.

To this background, we see that the *Lysis* agrees to some extent with the *Apology* about right. What the *Lysis* does not say, however, is that the non-good should pursue the relevant educational relations with various others. It does not seem to explicitly rule out that the non-good can identify who the good are in advance of searching for them from among a wider set of candidates. It suggests this, however, if chapter 3 above was correct that even in this dialogue only the good can identify good (or the good). Hence, the non-good can be utterly deceived as to who or what is good. To them the bad may seem good and the good bad. So perhaps the *Lysis* agrees with the *Apology* to a great extent though it does not say that the non-good ought to seek lessons from all others.

6.7. Moral Objections

Socrates' view of right seems immoral for at least two reasons. First, one is likelier to learn about good from the intelligent, so one does better to do right to the intelligent than to the non-intelligent. But one should do right to all, for all are equal from a moral viewpoint.

Second, cross-examining others is suited only to some situations. If someone is e.g. drowning it is inappropriate and indeed immoral to try to philosophize with them. But if right is an extrinsic end (see chapter 5), then it is to be done in relation to all external contexts, hence also in relation to the drowning.

Replies to the first objection: Grasping or applying Socrates' criteria does not seem to require special intelligence. His terms are ordinary, his explanations are brief, and he illustrates his views by invoking examples from everyday life. Moreover, even interlocutors who cannot apply Socrates' criteria have a role in

Socrates' procedure, for that procedure depends on hypotheses. Socrates himself cites e.g. poems. These do not need to teach of good in any obvious way, for they may turn out to do so only once they have been properly assessed.

More generally, for Socrates people who view the world differently from us are of special interest to us. *This* may be his general rule regarding how one should select one's interlocutors, not intelligence. Socrates seems in fact to go by something like it, for he poses his questions to inexperienced youths in the *Lysis* and the *Charmides*, and Ion, Hippias, and Euthyphro are clearly not the brightest persons he could find. Perhaps they are rather persons whose behaviour Socrates was least likely in his own view to be able to understand or predict. Perhaps that is why he selected them. Whether or not it is, we do know that intelligence is not his criterion.

(*Doing* right does not seem to require special intelligence either. Indeed, doing right is precisely a way to confess to a lack of special knowledge or ability.)

A reply to the second objection above: Socrates' philosophy is not meant to contain or address all of value, even of moral value. For we should not absurdly think of him as saying that one should always philosophize, for surely one needs to sleep and do other things also. Socrates' concern is specifically with what can be taught or policed, or with pure versus applied ethics. It is directed at our waking hours. (Perhaps it can be construed also as implying that we should maximize the share of such waking hours, in our own lives and also in everyone else's, but I have not attempted to show this here.) At any rate, Socrates need not be taken as meaning that the drowning should be philosophized with instead of being saved by means of physical action any more than he needs to be viewed as prohibiting sleep.

6.8. An Interpretive Objection

The possible worlds that Socrates invokes when measuring whether x is right are not all of them compatible with the idea that right has to do with edification. For example, what is temperate should be valuable when boxing *(Charmides 159C), but boxing surely is not instructive about good. Conversely, if even boxing is instructive about good then what is not? Socratic right becomes so wide in meaning that it fails to work as a sanction, because it excludes so few things.*

I am nearly powerless against this objection, and all I can say in defence of my interpretation is that Socrates probably does not really mean to propagate any kind of *boxing*—given that he is for the examined life—and that his reference to boxing might hence be but one among many of his illustrative analogies which he draws to achieve understandability but which he does not mean to be taken literally. After all, he does not predicate good of cooking either though he brings up cooking as a relevant normative example (see 3.2.).

6.9. Summary

In this chapter (6) we saw that for Socrates in the *Apology*, doing right is a matter of seeking correction about good (6.1.). This view of right seemed to satisfy the criteria described in chapters 4 and 5 (6.2.). It found some support in numerous other dialogues (6.3.-6.6.), and it seemed at least potentially to survive some moral and interpretive objections (6.7., 6.8.).

Notes

1. In which case, what is one's end? It is to attain a better or even a perfect end, and without knowing in advance what to count as better or perfect. (This can sound in some respects like the paradox of inquiry in the *Euthydemus* (275D-278C) and the *Meno* (80D-E).) For how is one to know what sort of a map to use in seeking an end which one cannot identify even in principle? And how could one care to want anything that one cannot even picture?

The means to be used are sincere questionings, so I will explain below in the main text, because these are the only means available to agents even if their internal powers do not help them to positive answers. *They* have no other means to escape their internal helplessness, so they face no choice. They must exhibit curiosity.

But what then do they aim at? If they do not have any conception of good at all they do not initially seek good in particular. They leap into the dark. But if they are lucky enough to find worthwhile interlocutors then their studies may soon inevitably come to concern good in particular. In that case they might say at this later stage in their process that they simply did not know what they were aiming at early on but that it none the less really was good, as they now know, having come closer to it. I am not sure that this is tenable.

On the other hand perhaps the right have some kind of a vague intuition of good before they begin to seek it, e.g. an innate one. This would perhaps be in the spirit of e.g. the *Meno*, the *Phaedo*, and the *Symposium*, for in these dialogues agents are driven towards aims they do not initially well understand. The right process would be one in which the intuition would be gradually clarified and ultimately this would mean its full-blooded instantiation as in chapters 2 and 3.

2. Observe that Socrates' solution is not reached by analyzing his problem but that it none the less solves that problem quite definitely. The problem is that the non-good cannot know their way forward (towards good), so they are intrinsically helpless. This does not *imply* that they need to seek help from others. But if they seek help from others then they quite definitely no longer need necessarily to suffer from their intrinsic helplessness. So the problems and the criteria (i.e. the solutions, or the routes to the solutions) apply on an analytical basis but they are not attained simply by analyzing already familiar problems or criteria. I am unable to generalize how they are attained.

3. But should one really seek to learn from persons instead of e.g. philosophy books? Are not the persons one meets liable to err more than textbooks? In Plato's early dialogues persons regularly receive better criticism from other persons than from poems or individual crafts. This applies also to Socrates, who is refuted by e.g. Callicles, see 2.4. He is also criticized in more ways than he seemed to have been able to expect in the *Charmides*.

There are a number of speculative points that can be made about Socrates' possibly plausible assumptions as reflected in passages like these. For instance, ordinary agents may often be less predictable than textbooks. Hence they may be more difficult to judge by their "covers" than books (which are always in specific *fields*, e.g., and have *titles*). Second, persons unlike books react to one's own views. Thus as a bookworm it is comparatively easy to come to think that one understands books and other persons and is clear-headed and self-sufficient because nobody ever comes along to say that one lacks these properties. One is oneself made an object (versus a subject) of attention only in intercourse with others, one can argue.

4. Precisely how long is a hypothesis allowed to remain seemingly obscure? 15 minutes? 2 pages? This is a difficult question, of course, as it seems hard to set any non-arbitrary limits.

5. Why does one need three levels instead of two? In chapter 4 it was said that the standard of right must be independent of right acts. But right acts in turn cannot be identified with first-order conceptions of good because these are not (always) agents who are free to disbelieve them; so if we dropped the second order from in between the third and the first then agents could not be required to do right independently of their context. There must be something which *chooses* to obey the third or the first order and is neither of them.

6. A complication for this hypothesis is that Socrates clearly is not always sincere for sometimes he is ironic. So if to do right is to do what he does then to do right is not always to be sincere. I would stress two qualifications in response to this.

First, Socrates is ironic typically when he needs to attain access to someone who shows no desire of doing right, i.e. of respecting others' free thought. He then uses ironic flattery, cunningly bringing his self-important interlocutors to take the time to express their views to him. (The flattery suits their self-important self-images and their aims of attaining social merit.) But whenever access has been attained and things get serious perhaps Socrates is sincere. This is an immensely difficult generalization to argue for, however, for it demands a survey of the all of the early dialogues and it is often a live issue whether he is being sincere or ironic. (It is indeed often especially difficult to tell which is being instantiated in a literary text.)

Second, in the *Apology* Socrates definitely seems sincere and this is the dialogue in which he most fully outlines his view of right. It may be admitted that all of the early Platonic dialogues do not exhibit the same conception of right. E.g. the *Ion* may not contain a view of right at all. Perhaps it is e.g. only comparatively late in his philosophizing career that the Socrates of the early dialogues notices that virtue (right) is something he has been exhibiting all along, by inquiring into it and into good. If so, then perhaps he is sincere whenever he has attained access to his interlocutor and he already conceives of right as in the *Apology*—which is perhaps the case *only* in this dialogue. But in it he seems sincere. None the less, several other dialogues can contain *similar* conceptions of right, and I will argue that this is so in later sections of this chapter (6).

7. This is not necessarily so regarding good. My view would be that he has only criteria of good but no conception or example of it. But it may be that I have merely not inspected the pragmatics of the early dialogues closely enough.

8. I ignore worlds in which nobody else happens to be around. (Is one e.g. to pretend that there is someone else there in them?)

9. But is it at all realistic to expect that wrong-doers' ways are reformed by means of Socratic education? Socrates does not claim it is, for he does not mean that this is an effective means of punishment but a just one; he is an ethician and not a psychologist.

10. To understand that this is not paradoxical, imagine a Cartesian philosopher of mind saying to an agent A that when A says x and claims incorrigibility, x is corrigible because A is wrong to think that x is a mental self-attribution. A may falsely believe that incorrigibility extends, say, to biology. The scope of incorrigibility is not itself an affair about which there is always incorrigibility.

11. Plato probably intends to present Socrates' as a kind of just court of law. The Athenian court condemns him to death because he is just, so the irony is perfect. For Athenians see Socrates' crime as consisting of his cross-examining activity, which is exactly what makes him just.

Chapter 7

SOCRATES AND THE *PHAEDO*

In this chapter (7) I will compare Socrates' views as these were presented in chapters 1-6 with those Plato presents as "Socrates'" in the *Phaedo*.[1] As noted in 0, I will refer to the ideas of these three dialogues as Plato's or SOCRATES' to distinguish them from those presented in 1-6 (Socrates'). (This is not a claim about the historical Socrates because I do not argue that any of Plato's views are the historical Socrates', see 0.) In the next chapter, 8, I will discuss SOCRATES' views in the *Theaetetus*.

SOCRATES' positions in both of these later than early dialogues differ from Socrates'. But I mean to highlight that they differ from Socrates only to a limited extent and that they differ from him in contrasting ways. The commonalities are that ends are self-predicated and that they are attained by social discourse. If this is correct, SOCRATES stays true to the basic Socratic teachings.[2]

7.1. The *Phaedo* on Good

In the *Phaedo* the "Forms" seem to be both (i) the only bearers of intrinsic value and (ii) self-predicated. But in contrast with Socratically good things as I have viewed them they (iii) do not evolve.

(i) In the *Phaedo* the aim of philosophers, or more specifically of their psyches, is to reach "Hades." This is the best place to be and it contains the Forms (67A-B, 80D-81A). Besides them, it contains the psyches of those who have lived well (or right, see 7.2. below) (67A). It has intrinsic value, SOCRATES means.

But what exactly then has intrinsic value? As noted, I will describe in (ii) how the Forms are self-predicated. SOCRATES has numerous terms of praise for the Forms throughout the dialogue. Psyches (in their ideal states), too, receive detailed attention and they are often praised in terms similar to those used in praise of the Forms. This leaves us with at least two options as to what SOCRATES now views as good. Is it only the Forms or is it psyches' contacts with the Forms (and with each other)?

The second alternative leaves things quite vague because SOCRATES does not much describe the way in which psyches connect or unite with Forms in this dialogue. Clearly psyches can value the Forms and they can seek some sort of contact with them (see e.g. 67A-B) but what exactly is this sought after contacting relation? SOCRATES does not appear to say that psyches can become identical to the Forms or that psyches can instantiate Forms, for example. Despite this he recurrently assigns similar or the same properties to both Forms and psyches, e.g. simplicity (78B-84B). Perceptual terms (see e.g. 74B-C) do not tell us how psyches and Forms can relate because they are not to be taken literally, empirically (65E-66A).

But we do not face a similar problem if we view SOCRATES as predicating good only of the Forms. For he says, as I will argue below in (ii) (in this section, 7.1.), that they are distinct relations (or relatings) and this answers the question how they relate with anything. The Forms *are* answers precisely to such questions because the Forms are relations. A second advantage of predicating good of them is that they relate intrinsically. For they relate in perfectly satisfactory ways only to themselves, and this can be taken as the aspect due to which they have intrinsic value. This is why we should prefer to view only the Forms as intrinsically valuable in the *Phaedo*. If we do this then we find in it a theory of good. Conversely, if we say that in it good things consist of relations between psyches and Forms then the dialogue does not contain an explicit position regarding good.

In 7.2. I will be describing right in the *Phaedo* and then I will try to show that psyches' attempted contacts with other things are right. It is reasonably clear in what *attempts* to reach the Forms can consist in even if the reachings are not easy to understand. In this way, psyches will have a place in the *Phaedo*'s ethic though good is not predicated of them.

(ii) In the *Phaedo*, the Forms are self-predicated in that at 74B-D they are both general standards and things which satisfy those standards better than other things do. For here SOCRATES says that there is only one fully equal thing (74D; this I will call a "Form") but that it is this thing which guides us in finding even apparent, occasional, or approximate equalities in other things such as sticks and stones (74C). So a single thing is both a standard and a superlative instance on that standard, both at once.[3] This seems to be meant as a general point about the Forms in the *Phaedo*, so that one would find Forms other than the Equal to self-instantiate in an analogical manner.

Besides being self-predicated, the Forms in the *Phaedo* never appear other than they are (74B-C). This may be a way to say that they are self-evident. I.e., whatever x is a Form of, x will reveal this information in a quite obvious way or it will not be a Form at all. So one cannot fasten on a Form and then be confused about it. If one is confused, uncertain, about something then one's object is not a Form.

So far, the Forms are self-predicated and self-evident. These properties connect naturally because self-predicated things are general standards, so they provide evidence for things. Moreover, self-predicated things also satisfy their standards better than other things do, so it is precisely for themselves that they provide their best evidence, and in this sense they are self-evident.

This dialogue also seems to say that Forms are primitive or at least simple (partless) (78B-84B). This may be implied by self-predication (and self-evidence) for if x relates only to x then x does not relate to y (if x≠y), so seemingly x needs to be separable from all other things to qualify as self-predicated and if it is separable then it is primitive.

A fourth feature of the Forms in the *Phaedo* seems to be their causal effectiveness (105B-C). They alter things into their own shapes, so e.g. Equality would make things more equal than before. This relates to a fifth property of the Forms, namely their being particulars not universals; for the presence of a universal, heat, in a particular does not explain its hotness but rather its contact with a particular fire does (ibid.). The point seems to be not about the nature of explanation but about causation, for now things are moved only by particular events, not by their kinds.

Sixth, the Forms are ethical forces, for efficient causes are final ones (98D-99C) and we just noted that the Forms are efficient (fifth property). Forms seem in the *Phaedo* to be primitive causally and ethically at once (100B, 99C). One might hence think of them, somewhat paradoxically, as both the original springs of things as well as their destinations. The idea of a return to origins repeats throughout the dialogue (think of the doctrines of reincarnation and recollection), so this connection seems to be an intended one.

SOCRATES' examples of Forms do not always sound ethical, however: we already met with equality and heat. A perfectly hot thing, whatever that is, does not sound like a particularly good one. Perhaps examples like these are meant only as illustrations and in a literal sense all Forms are for good contents only, but this is speculative.

All of the above six features of the Forms are features of good things for Socrates in the earlier Platonic dialogues. But in (i) we saw that Plato seems to mean that the Forms alone are intrinsically valuable. So the SOCRATES of the *Phaedo* seems to agree with Socrates' views on good. These figures pick out good things on roughly the same criteria.

(iii) Next, some differences between the *Phaedo*'s view and Socrates'. I will first note a few that seem to be less important and then I will come to one that seems to be worth highlighting.

A first apparent difference is that the *Phaedo* says there are many Forms, but Socrates does not speak of good*s*. He speaks of good. On the other hand, Socrates does not seem to mean that only a single particular in history can be good. What he does seem to mean is that we are to have a single criterion of good and that various different things can and ought to meet that criterion. Indeed, he obviously tries to get others to try for goodness and he seemed to predicate good of acts they might perform at some future time if things go well. Yet he never even alludes to the alternative of a single collective action as being good. So seemingly good is a single kind and its instances are many (indeed perhaps as many as possible). So we should not be too quick to say that SOCRATES and Socrates actually disagree as to the plurality of good.[4]

A second difference between Socrates and the *Phaedo* can seem to be that SOCRATES never seems to say that agents can become or instantiate the Forms, nor that the Forms are agents. But Socrates predicated good of activities in chapter 3, and so perhaps for Socrates an agent can become good but for SOCRATES one cannot. But as noted in (i) the *Phaedo*'s psyches are praised in terms used of the Forms also and psyches and Forms seem to share at least the property of being simple. Another reason to question the Form/psyche distinction (or its relevance to the *Phaedo*'s ethics) is that the Forms do for their part at least vaguely resemble (rational) agents in that they are particulars with causal powers and reasons. It seems warranted to conclude that the *Phaedo* does not really tell us clearly whether the Forms are agents *or not*. For it divorces them from psyches but gives them properties of agents.

Third, in the *Phaedo* the Forms do not seem to evolve but Socrates said that good things evolve (see chapter 3 above). For in the *Phaedo* the Forms effect changes in things other than themselves, but the dialogue seems to contain no hint that they change themselves in the same or similar ways.[5] This seems like a notable difference, for now the SOCRATES of the *Phaedo* seems ultimately to be praising rest where the Socrates of the earlier dialogues praised activity. (The *Phaedo*'s conception of good seems hence to fall by the "paradox of the will" described in 2.6.)

In sum of 7.1., the SOCRATES of Plato's *Phaedo* agrees largely but not wholly with the early dialogues' Socrates on good.

7.2. The *Phaedo* on Right

All agents should philosophize whenever possible, SOCRATES seems to say in the *Phaedo*. For philosophical (wisdom-loving) value finds a competitor (or many competitors) only in empirically oriented (bodily) value and the latter should be ignored as often and as completely as possible. This general evaluation is made at e.g. 67A-B where SOCRATES notes that bodily forces will only obstruct us (67A) from our liberated aim. We (or our "psyches," souls) need purification from them, he says. Such purification seems for him to be an alternative available to all (73A). So there is a single kind of choice open to everyone between purist freedom and bodily imprisonment and confusion.

But why are these *the* options and why is it so clear that the one needs to be ranked above the other? Not because of any everyday familiarity with the division or the ranking. For in everyday life the map of values does not seem this reduced, SOCRATES says. Everyday views are in fact for him too often representative of the bodily alternative. They should be replaced by the simple and philosophical alternative. They are not the authority for this decision.

More concretely, in everyday life one speaks of diverse virtues, each suited to particular types of circumstance and none to all. SOCRATES seems to want to retain this scope for evaluative attitudes but to reduce their complexity. Why? At 68D-69A he says that it is contradictory to be courageous towards something because one is more fearful of something else (68D) or to abstain from certain pleasures for the sake of other pleasures (68E-69A). Where is the contradiction? Apparently it occurs when desired things belong to the same kind as those which are resisted. For it is not really the same particulars that seem to be wanted and not wanted in the above cases. Rather they are merely too alike. So common aims fail of distinctness. One would avoid this contradiction, one supposes, by seeking things that are distinct from others in kind.

But SOCRATES sees also a second problem with everyday virtues and this tells us that it is not exactly distinctness in sought after ends that makes the difference. For at 69A-C the fault of everyday virtues seems to be that the currency of the exchanges made in them is not the same as or similar enough to the objects exchanged for on that currency. For both the coin (69A) and the objects traded for by using it (69C) should be "wisdom." (Pleasures and fears should not amount to much on this currency (69A).) So the currency should not in fact be used for anything external to itself (69C). Hence it would be a measure for other things (negatively) and also such as measure only itself in an affirming way. This sounds a great deal like self-predication.

But now we have seen two seemingly different faults in ordinary virtues. To demand ends that are distinct in kind from other things may not be to demand ends that are measured by themselves (or by things much like themselves). We can view the requirement of distinctness as a preliminary for the self-predication requirement, however, if the intended distinctness is not only in standards but also in ends. If we do not view SOCRATES' meaning in this way then seemingly we need to view him as making two incompatible demands. It seems to be a more charitable option to say that he requires distinctness of aims and standards and that the distinctness in both cases is the same. If so, the ends he propagates are self-predicated.

But if so, is SOCRATES now requiring that philosophers or philosophizing should be distinct and self-predicated? Not quite. For what he actually propagates is the *effort to find* distinct and self-predicated things. It is not up to him, he says, to succeed in finding them (69C-D). Indeed there is no guarantee that such things can even be attained at all (85C-E, 90E). It is only the effort that he can make out of his own resources. He also seems to believe in the *Phaedo* that others can freely follow this prescription (at 73A, as noted). Purification is, we should think, a voluntary process open to agents generally. Success at it is another matter. But SOCRATES seems also to think that without the effort the success is impossible, as if voluntary efforts in the purification process were a necessary but insufficient means to (or condition of) the aim.[6]

So philosophers seek aims which are distinct and self-predicated and in doing so they instantiate some kind of value. But how is it that philosophers seek these sorts of aims? I.e. what is their characteristic activity? If we can find this out then perhaps we can see what kind of value philosophers exhibit in their characteristic efforts.

They attempt to learn from *other agents* about distinct and self-predicated things (namely the Forms and some other related things such as the psyche). For the philosophizing which SOCRATES practices and preaches consists of mutual questioning by distinct persons. So purification is social.[7]

All this is to speak of a category of value which is not intrinsic. It is predicated of what relates to things other than itself and what thereby seeks what is self-predicated. It has value in all kinds of different contexts (because it replaces the plural everyday virtues, see above) and it is open, seemingly, to all. But it is also quite reduced in that it is not complex as the ordinary virtues are though it covers the same area of value as they do. It is reduced in that it consists of seeking correction by purer views. That and that alone decides whether one has this kind of value or not. But these were properties of right in 4-6, so the *Phaedo* seems to agree with the early dialogues about right.

Here are a few objections to this thesis.

First, one might argue that the early dialogues do not feature the *Phaedo*'s asceticism, i.e. its opposition to bodily pleasures, for they seem rather to attack e.g. vain self-importance or boastfulness, which seem like social vices. However, this does not seem like a great contrast because these two kinds of evil seem to be judged as evils on similar criteria in the *Phaedo* as in the earlier dialogues. Moreover, neither viewpoint seems to claim to have the correct theory of evils, for both claim, after all, that evils share the feature of being *difficult* to theorize. They are indistinct, passive, plural, etc. So according to both viewpoints there can probably be very many different theories of evils and all will be at most approximate. To this background, these two viewpoints do not seem to be in any important disagreement about evils.

Second, it is possible to argue that the *Phaedo* values consistency more than Socrates does and, conversely, that Socrates values, as right, efforts to be corrected by others, not any (other) consistency. In support of this it can be said that the *Phaedo* is a discussion among like-minded thinkers whereas Socrates tends to converse with characters he fails to understand. For Simmias and Cebes agree with SOCRATES on major points (see e.g. 74B-E) but Socrates' interlocutors typically do not. Socrates' interlocutors can fail to understand him utterly (compare Ion, Hippias, Euthyphro) or disagree with him most radically (Thrasymachus, Callicles). Also, the *Phaedo* does recurrently praise such things as harmony and consistency (e.g. 80B) and conversely it does not contain similar enthusiasm for refutations or paradoxes as the early dialogues did (think especially of the *Gorgias* and the *Apology*). Lastly, we already saw in 7.1. that the *Phaedo* seems ultimately to praise rest, i.e. a consistency in time, and of course one of its main conclusions is for a kind of dying (e.g. 66E).

This objection seems to be correct but we should not overemphasize it. For SOCRATES denies that he has certain knowledge (e.g. 85C-E, 90E) and he does not mean to condemn the critical powers of human agents in general (73A). He is still looking for more perfect views from others or with their help. Right remains something one should instantiate day and night until one attains good and it is about receiving edification from others in direct dialogue.

In sum of 7.2., the *Phaedo* seems to agree roughly with Socrates about right.

7.3. Summary

In this chapter (7) we found SOCRATES to agree with Socrates about good (7.1.) and right (7.2.) to a large extent. There were a few exceptions regarding both topics, however. Good no longer appeared as dynamic and right now seemed to have more to do with maintaining consistent discipline than with trying to come by unexpected revisions.

Notes

1. The *Phaedo* is today commonly taken to be a middle phase dialogue in Plato's writing career and the *Theaetetus* is viewed as late, see Fine, "Introduction" p. 1n1. I do not aim to support or to contradict this historical categorization of Plato's dialogues.

2. In a longer discussion of the *Phaedo* and the *Theaetetus*, it would be worthwhile to look for Platonic improvements on Socrates. This I do not attempt to do here. My aim all along in this essay is to illuminate and to defend Socrates based on what he says. The discussion of chapters 7 and 8 contributes to this end if Plato's middle-phase agreement with Socrates counts as supportive of Socrates.

3. What can this Form equate with? If it is a single thing, as SOCRATES seems to mean, then presumably it would be nonsense to equate it with anything other than itself. Perhaps he means that it is the only perfectly self-identical thing. If so, then other Forms mentioned in this dialogue would fail of self-identity in *its* sense. This would leave one wondering how distinct each Form can be from the rest and how many there are.

But this is just one of many questions that can be raised about the *Phaedo* which I will not deal with in this chapter (7), for my aim is not to assess its plausibility per se but only to compare its position with the earlier dialogues' Socrates'.

4. In pursuing this comparison further one would need to say how distinct the *Phaedo*'s Forms are from each other and likewise how distinct Socrates' good acts are from each other.

5. The *Phaedo* does seem to imply that Forms alter themselves also if it says that (a) the Forms alter things, (b) each Form relates to whatever it relates to in a single way, and (c) the Forms relate also to themselves (they are self-predicated). (b) may be wrong because perhaps the self-relations of the Forms are special, i.e. unlike their relations to other things.

6. This is I think the main message of the *Phaedo*. Certainty about the Forms and about the (immortal) nature of the psyche is to be *sought* and such seeking activity is propagated. On this view, the import of this dialogue is mainly ethical, for it aims to tell us how to live. Then its central message would not be that the psyche is immortal or that the Forms exist.

No certainty is claimed in this dialogue that Forms (or immortal psyches) can be secured as ends (see 7.2. below). One must bravely face the risk, aiming high without guarantees of success. The price paid in taking this risk is of course in earthly (bodily) goods. The high-minded ethic can turn out to be illusory, and so perhaps eventually this price will be paid for nothing.

On the other hand, SOCRATES does not view this risky state of things as necessarily more than temporary, for though he is unsure of his various hypotheses he entertains hopes that they could be secured through philosophizing, see 90E. So perhaps one day the risking element will disappear. (Yet seemingly then right would disappear also as then the search for good (or for Forms or for immortal psyches) would be over. I am not sure how SOCRATES views this prospect.)

7. Here I cannot resist asking why: Why is purification social in the *Phaedo*? Its end-points, the Forms, are not social unless they are agents. But nor hence are its standards (due to self-predication). Neither is communicative, e.g. responsive to questions. In that case it seems like one might as well look to sticks and stones (see 7.1.) for knowledge about the Forms as to other persons. Neither sticks nor persons will be self-predicated or communicative of good anyway. Not so if the good are agents. In 7.1. it was left open whether they are that in the *Phaedo*.

Chapter 8

SOCRATES AND THE *THEAETETUS*

As already declared in the introduction to chapter 7, this chapter (8) compares the views of the "Socrates" (SOCRATES) of the *Theaetetus* with those of the Socrates of the earlier dialogues (discussed in chapters 1-6).

We will find agreement on major points. Where SOCRATES now fails explicitly to endorse the earlier dialogues' views, however, he also happens to fail explicitly to endorse the *Phaedo*'s. Hence we can say that in these two non-early dialogues SOCRATES does not turn against the earlier dialogues' views in a single, consistent way (when at all).

8.1. The *Theaetetus* on Good

The *Theaetetus* is concerned with the nature of knowledge. If this end were attained, it is implied, it would be known what knowledge is. Hence, the end sought in this dialogue is in a sense "self-predicated." For there is on the one hand a measure (for knowledge) and then something that satisfies that measure (knowledge of what knowledge is), but these two descriptions apply to a single thing. In other words, the second order predicate ("x knows") is now applied to itself ("x knows that x knows," or "x knows what knowing is"), providing the second order with a first order for it to apply to *from itself*.

I will now list some more detailed points on which the *Theaetetus*' SOCRATES seems to agree with Socrates and then reply to objections to this assimilation. My aim is not any complete survey of this complex dialogue.

First, the identification of any instance of a property of the relevant sort (knowledge) depends on the identification of a self-predicated instance of it (knowledge of knowledge), for one could not know about shoes if one did not first know about knowledge (147B; also see 146E).

This epistemological priority is familiar from Socrates. For if one must first know what knowledge is and only then come to be an expert about shoes then one could not possibly discover what knowledge is by asking ordinary craftspersons, e.g. shoemakers, about this (or by studying their traits in other ways). This is so at least unless they happened to be epistemologists, but in that case it would not matter whether they are e.g. shoemakers also. But it is obvious that SOCRATES does not mean that shoemakers characteristically are epistemologists. Hence he does not want to reach his self-predicated aim by studying the crafts of his day. Rather he wants at most to be somehow inspired by them in his idealizations and to use them as imperfect analogues to communicate his meaning. This allows him to view as knowledge something which ordinary craftspersons do not recognize as such.[1]

If knowledge is attained only by first attaining a self-predicated instance of it, then it cannot be attained by examining the crafts and generalizing from there. Given this, it is possible for ordinary views, exhibited in e.g. the crafts, to err entirely about knowledge.[2]

Second, an expert concerning x can produce or reproduce x.[3] For an expert about visual similarity can *draw* (154A). She must be e.g. a painter (ibid.). So an expert about x is not merely aware of x or of x's differences with various or all non-x's. Nor can she merely communicate something basic to x's nature to non-experts in a neutral language. For the precise way in which she manifests her expertise about x is by producing or reproducing x. Accordingly, knowledge is a kind of action, and what knows is an agent, for to produce or reproduce something (intentionally) is to be an agent.

If knowledge is always a kind of action then so is knowledge of knowledge. So the epistemologist, or what is self-predicated in the *Theaetetus* (the knower about knowledge), is an agent.

The self-predicated aims of the *Phaedo*, the Forms, did not seem to be acts of agents (see 7.1.). Indeed, it does not seem that a Form might know what knowledge is. But Socrates' good things were agents in chapter 3. It would hence be misled to generalize that SOCRATES turns away from Socrates to a less action-oriented view of self-predication, for his view is Socratic on this score in the *Theaetetus*.[4]

Third, an expert concerning x concerns herself with the entire causal lifetime of x. If x were a plant, an expert about it would be aware of how x is planted, grown, and harvested (149E). Conversely, on this conception there are no experts of phases or aspects of things. Experts are concerned only with causally complete and distinct processes.

This suggests that experts' objects are causally individuated. If so, perhaps they are not individuated analytically, for analysis can lead one to logically separable parts that may not be causally separable. Conversely, perhaps some conceptual frameworks are not as fine-grained as causal entities are. If so, analysis of them might produce results that lack the required specificness.

A further implication seems to be that knowledge is known about in causal independence from other things if that self-predicated aim is attained at all. For if the object of an expert is causally independent and now the expert is her own object then seemingly she is causally independent. This would accord with Socrates' assertion of the causal independence of the good in chapter 3.

Fourth, at least sometimes SOCRATES seems to individuate things teleologically. For at 176E-177A he describes two kinds of lifestyle, one philosophical and the other unreasoned. The negative acts characteristic of the second decide what punishments are deserved and received by them. For the acts and the reactions to them are alike to each other in this passage. So it is as if it were in the very nature of the acts in question to receive certain evaluative reactions. If this is *all* there is to their nature then they seem to be individuated teleologically, for then acts will be (like) their aims.

This is similar to Socratic views familiar from chapters 2 and 3 but it is now stated about evils and not about good things. This is puzzling because in chapters 2 and 3 the evaluative and productive self-relation was claimed to be found only in good things and not in bad or evil ones. Also, above in this section (8.1.) we saw SOCRATES maintaining that experts produce copies of their objects, and now it seems to be implied that evil or bad figures do so also, though they do not appear to be treated now as experts. None the less, we have here a thought similar in structure to Socrates' and that is all I mean to claim.

Now I will turn to two objections to the above assimilations of the early dialogues' Socrates with the SOCRATES of the *Theaetetus*.

First, at 148D SOCRATES seems to be for an analytical procedure for he tells Theaetetus merely to find what is common and specific to a set of things that are accepted as cases or areas of knowledge from ordinary life. If SOCRATES thought thus, he would base on and not seek to reform everyday norms. This would mean that he disagrees with Socrates as I interpreted him (though also with the *Phaedo*, see 7).

As against this objection, we need to note that the above passage may stand for a merely preliminary stage in SOCRATES' favoured process. Perhaps it is worthwhile to *begin* with commonalities and differences between ordinary things, or by relating alternative norms to those everyday continuities and differences. Moreover, if SOCRATES does mean to base on ordinary intuitions or practices then at least some of the above four features of epistemologists described earlier in this section (8.1.) could not be consistently demanded, for all of these four features do not seem to be found in e.g. shoemaking (e.g. the first). They would be without foundation if foundations had to be familiar from ordinary crafts. Hence SOCRATES seems more consistent if he does not claim his norms to be necessarily familiar from everyday life. But then his basis is not only analytical.[5]

Second, unlike the earlier dialogues' hero the SOCRATIC philosopher can seem to aim at an impartial and general viewpoint. For at 173E-174B SOCRATES sees the philosopher being for general and descriptive studies and not, like Socrates, for focus and reform. For he says that characteristically a philosopher will look to the stars and not see what is at her feet, and that she will think of general topics continually and not even know her neighbour. But Socrates got to know his neighbours and his concerns were not very broad but only specifically ethical.

But this view is oddly out of tune with SOCRATES' main project in this dialogue, which does not consist of finding a general picture of things but rather specifically of attaining knowledge about knowledge, for the sake of which he was found earlier in this section (8.1.) to make idealizations. But seemingly it is safer to view his sincere position as represented in the longer and arguably main discussion rather than in this brief note. If so, SOCRATES is for a largely Socratic view: philosophers are focused reformers, not surveyors of the most general aspects of things.

But then it is puzzling that SOCRATES says what he just did. I do admit that things are not very smoothly in favour of the early Socrates in the *Theaetetus*. Because the dialogue seems so heterogenous it appears that cases can be made both ways, for and against Socrates. But I would note that the cases made above on the "for" side are for their part not without force.

In sum of 8.1., in the *Theaetetus* SOCRATES aims at becoming (and aiding his interlocutors to become) self-predicated and he views that end as causally active and as distinct, and this is to aim at something similar to what Socrates viewed as good in chapter 3.

8.2. The *Theaetetus* on Right

In the *Theaetetus* Plato's SOCRATES seeks answers to his questions from others (on a self-predicated topic, as just explained in 8.1.). He only asks, he does not answer. The positive results are his interlocutors', he says (150D, 161B; see also 148E-151D, 210B-C). He approaches his interlocutors with questions and not only with hypothetical answers. He is open to lessons from them. He also never forces his interlocutor's reaction. So he seems to do right roughly in the sense of chapters 4-6.

On the other hand, SOCRATES does not seem to say in the *Theaetetus* that social inquiry is the single and general "extrinsic end" in the sense described in chapter 5. For he does not appear to say that social inquiry into what is self-predicated has value in all (negative) contexts. No passage in this dialogue seems to indicate ways in which social philosophizing might be a way to confront various evils in different contexts. Due to this, we cannot say that SOCRATES adopts all of Socrates' main views on right.[6]

But to the extent that he does not praise philosophical studies as an extrinsic end he fails to agree not only with the earlier dialogues' Socrates but also with the *Phaedo*, for in 7.2. we saw that on this score the *Phaedo* and the early dialogues were largely in agreement. So once again we have a basis to generalize that Plato's later than early dialogues do not depart from Socrates in any single and consistent way. They do not pursue things in a single anti-Socratic direction.

This applies also to a further point. For a difference specifically with the *Phaedo* is that in the *Theaetetus* SOCRATES is keener to expose inconsistencies and to find variety than to come to a consistent position comparatively soon. Here he seems to side with the earlier dialogues' Socrates against the *Phaedo*.

It seems warranted to conclude this section (8.2.) by stating that the *Theaetetus*' SOCRATES partly agrees with the earlier dialogues' Socrates about right and that in so far as he does not he contradicts the *Phaedo*'s position also.

8.3. Summary

In this chapter (8) the *Theaetetus* was found to support several of the earlier dialogues' views on good (8.1.) and right (8.2.). In so far as it did not it seemed to contradict the *Phaedo* (discussed in 7).

Notes

1. *Why* does SOCRATES require knowledge about knowledge first? Is it correct that a non-epistemologist never knows about shoes? As against this, it could be that there are several different kinds of knowledge and that the kind familiar to the shoemaker (however non-intellectually and practically) is perfectly satisfactory as applied specifically to *shoes* (even if not to other things). This is what a contextualist such as DeRose might say.

I will not be concerned with why-questions regarding the *Theaetetus*, for the pursuit of answers to these would be overwhelmingly complex for this brief discussion of this dialogue.

2. This implied, for the Socrates of the earlier dialogues, that the search for self-predicated instances needs to be radically open-minded (see chapter 6). Craft-knowledge needs to be more or less familiar from everyday life for Socrates to be able to refer to it in his analogies.

Things would be very different if the crafts exhibited the kind of knowledge that Socrates is after. In that case, one would not need to enquire about it from strangers in general, and one would focus one's inquiries only on craftspersons in particular. But this is not what Socrates does. If he did do that, or say that one should do that, then a humane aspect of his ethic would fall away.

3. Or *does* she draw instead of merely being able to? If she were good in Socrates' sense she would (see chapter 3). But here I ignore nuances such as this one.

4. If an expert produces a copy of her object and an epistemologist is an expert about her own kind of activity, does the epistemologist produce a copy of her own type of action? What would this mean? This seems to be implied but I do not think that any idea like this is explained in the *Theaetetus*.

5. My own suspicion is that analysis or the drawing of analogies between things familiar from ordinary life has a preliminary role in both procedures, Socrates' and the *Theaetetus*', and that the more essential work is not analytical but causal and ethical.

6. The dialogue does close with a note that if Theaetetus is aware that he lacks authority (about something concerning which he should have it) then he is more bearable to his fellow humans (210C). Perhaps the thought is that he is then more likely to ask questions of others than to seek to manipulate them or to ignore them.

But this is only a short note. This is not to say the more general thing that social inquiry (into what is self-predicated) has value in all (negative) contexts.

CONCLUSION

I have sought in this book to defend a libertarian view of Socrates and simultaneously with that a Socratic view of liberty.

On this view Socrates' characteristic quest for definitions of ends is free in one sense while the sought definitions, or rather acts of defining, are free in another sense. The seeking consists of questioning others. It is a relation of external dependency. The defining, again, is fully self-sufficient, depending only on itself. Both of these things deserve to be thought of as free.

The connection between these two freedoms, here termed the good and the right kinds of freedom, was also described. One has reason to search for self-sufficiency if one does not have it (or one faces what was called the paradox of the will). One needs to search everywhere because one cannot know where to search. One cannot know where to search because, as one does know (avoiding the paradox of inquiry), what one searches for is self-relational. Because it is self-relational it is not known about in degrees. One has it or not: there are no degrees.

If this is correct then Socrates' search for definitions is essentially a practical effort. It is not a project in the philosophy of language, metaphysics, or general epistemology. It is essentially not even about trying to understand what has value or what is free. Rather, it is specifically the attempt to bear value, and to *be* free.

The above were the main ideas of the discussion in chapters 1-6. Chapters 7 and 8 noted in what ways Plato's middle and later dialogues affirm similar things.

BIBLIOGRAPHY

Adam, Charles, and Tannery, Paul, eds. *Oeuvres des Descartes*, revised edition, 12 volumes. Paris: J Vrin, 1964-1976.
Albritton, Rogers. "Freedom Of Will And Freedom Of Action", reprinted in Gary Watson (ed.), pp. 408-423.
Arendt, Hannah. *The Life Of The Mind*. New York: Harcourt Inc., 1978.
——. *The Origins of Totalitarianism*. New York: Harcourt, 1951.
Aristotle. *The Complete Works of Aristotle*, Jonathan Barnes (ed.). Princeton: Princeton University Press, 1984.
Ayer, A.J. *Language, Truth, And Logic*. London: Victor Gollancz, 1936.
Bealer, George. "The A Priori", in John Greco and Ernest Sosa (eds.), pp. 243-270.
Bentham, Jeremy. *Introduction To The Principles Of Morals And Legislation*. Oxford: Oxford University Press, 1907.
Beversluis, John. *Cross-Examining Socrates: A Defense Of The Interlocutors In Plato's Early Dialogues*. Cambridge: Cambridge University Press, 2000.
Blackburn, Simon. *Spreading The Word: Groundings In The Philosophy Of Language*. Oxford: Clarendon, 1984.
Brandt, Richard B. *A Theory Of The Good And The Right*. Amherst, N.Y.: Prometheus Books, 1979.
——. Ethical Theory: The Problems Of Normative And Critical Ethics. Englewood Cliffs: Prentice-Hall, 1959.
Brink, David O. *Moral Realism And The Foundations of Ethics*. New York: Cambridge University Press, 1989.
Campbell, Joseph Keim, O'Rourke, Michael, and Shier, David, eds. *Freedom And Determinism*. Cambridge, Mass.: MIT Press, 2004.
Campbell, Keith. *Abstract Particulars*. Oxford: Blackwell, 1990.
Chisholm, Roderick. *Perceiving: A Philosophical Study*. Ithaca: Cornell University Press, 1957.
Chomsky, Noam. *Language And Responsibility*. New York: Pantheon, 1979.
Dancy, Jonathan. *An Introduction To Contemporary Epistemology*. Oxford: Blackwell, 1985.
——. Ethics Without Principles. Oxford: Oxford University Press, 2004.
Davidson, Donald. *Inquiries Into Truth And Interpretation*. Oxford: Oxford University Press, 1984.
——. "On The Very Idea Of A Conceptual Scheme", reprinted in *Inquiries Into Truth And Interpretation*, pp. 183-198.
Davidson, Donald. *Essays On Actions And Events*. Oxford: Clarendon, 1980.
DeRose, Keith. "Contextualism: An Explanation And Defense", in John Greco and Ernest Sosa (eds.), 187-205.
Feyerabend, Paul K. *Problems Of Empiricism: Philosophical Papers,* Vol. 2. Cambridge: Cambridge University Press, 1981.
Fine, Gail. "Introduction", in: Gail Fine (ed.), *Plato*, Vol. I, pp. 3-14.
——, ed. Plato, 2 Vols. Oxford: Clarendon, 1999.
Foot, Philippa, ed. *Theories Of Ethics*. Oxford: Oxford University Press, 1967.
Fraenkel, Hermann. „A Thought Pattern In Heraclitus", reprinted in Alexander Mourelatos (ed.), pp. 101-114.
Geach, Peter. "Good And Evil", reprinted in Philippa Foot (ed.), 64-73.

Gilligan, Carol. *In A Different Voice: Psychological Theory And Women's Development.* Harvard: Harvard University Press, 1983.
Gosling. J. C. B. *Plato.* London: Routledge & Kegan Paul, 1983.
Greco, John & Sosa, Ernest, eds. *The Blackwell Guide To Epistemology.* Oxford: Blackwell, 1999.
Grene, David. *Greek Political Theory.* Chicago: University Of Chicago Press, 1965.
Griswold, Charles L., ed. *Platonic Writings, Platonic Readings.* New York: Routledge, Chapman & Hall, 1988.
Guthrie, W.C.K. *A History Of Greek Philosophy*, Vol. IV. Cambridge: Cambridge University Press, 1975.
Habermas, Jürgen. *Theorie des kommunikativen Handelns*, 2 Vols. Frankfurt a.M.: Suhrkamp, 1995.
Hamann, Johann Georg. *Sokratische Denkwürdigkeiten/Aesthetica in nuce*, ed. Sven-Aage Jörgenson. Stuttgart: Philipp Reclam Verlag, 1968.
Hare, Richard M. *The Language Of Morals.* Oxford: Oxford University Press, 1952.
Harsanyi, John. "Morality And The Theory Of Rational Behavior", reprinted in Amartya Sen et. al. (eds.), pp. 39-62.
Heidegger, Martin. *Sein und Zeit.* Tübingen: Niemeyer, 1993.
Hintikka, Jaakko. "*Cogito, Ergo Sum:* Inference Or Performance?", reprinted in Georges J. D. Moyal (ed.), pp. 162-184.
Hull, David L. *Philosophy Of Biological Science.* Englewood Cliffs: Prentice-Hall, 1974.
Hume, David. *A Treatise Of Human Nature*, ed. L.A. Selby-Bigge. Oxford: Clarendon Press, 1995.
Irwin, Terence. *Plato's Ethics.* Oxford: Oxford University Press, 1995.
——, ed. Plato's Metaphysics And Epistemology. New York: Garland Publishing Inc., 1995.
Jaeger, Werner. *Paideia: The Ideals Of Greek Culture,* 3 Vols, transl. Gilbert Highet. Oxford: Oxford University Press, 1944.
Jubien, Michael. *Contemporary Metaphysics.* Oxford: Blackwell, 1997.
Kane, Robert. „Responsibility, Luck, And Chance: Reflections On Free Will And Determinism", reprinted in Gary Watson (ed.), pp. 299-321.
Kant, Immanuel. *Gesammelte Schriften,* Vol. IV. Paul Menzer, ed. Berlin: Preussische Akademie der Wissenschaften, 1911.
Katz, Jerrold J. *Propositional Structure and Illocutionary Force.* New York: Crowell, 1977.
Kierkegaard, Søren. *Concluding Unscientific Postscript To* Philosophical Fragments, transl. Howard V. Hong and Edna H. Hong. Princeton: Princeton University Press, 1992.
——. *The Sickness Unto Death: A Christian Psychological Exposition Of Edification & Awakening*, transl. Alastair Hannay. London: Penguin, 1989.
Kraut, Richard, ed. *The Cambridge Companion To Plato.* Cambridge: Cambridge University Press, 1992.
Kripke, Saul. *Naming And Necessity.* Harvard: Harvard University Press, 1972.
Künne, Wolfgang. *Conceptions Of Truth.* Oxford: Oxford University Press, 2003.
Lewis, David. "Defining 'Intrinsic'", reprinted in David Lewis, pp. 116-132.
——. Papers In Metaphysics And Epistemology. Cambridge: Cambridge University Press, 1999.
Losee, John. *A Historical Introduction To The Philosophy Of Science.* Oxford: Oxford University Press, 1972.
Mackie, J.L. *Ethics: Inventing Right And Wrong.* Harmondsworth: Penguin, 1977.

Marx, Karl, ed. and transl. T.B. Bottomore. *Early Writings.* New York: McGraw-Hill, 1963.
McDowell, John. *Mind, Value, And Reality.* Cambridge, Mass.: Harvard University Press, 1998.
——. "Virtue And Reason", reprinted in Mind, Value, And Reality, pp. 50-73.
Meixner, Uwe, and Newen, Albert, eds. *Philosophiegeschichte und logische Analyse,* Vol. 8. Paderborn: Mentis, 2005.
Millikan, Ruth. *Language: A Biological Model.* Oxford: Oxford University Press, 2005.
Moore, G.E. "The Conception Of Intrinsic Value", reprinted in *Principia Ethica,* pp. 280-298.
——. "Free Will", reprinted in Principia Ethica, pp. 299-311.
——. Principia Ethica, 2nd ed. Cambridge: Cambridge University Press, 1994.
Moravcsik, Julius. *Plato And Platonism: Plato's Conception Of Appearance And Reality In Ontology, Epistemology And Ethics And Its Modern Echoes.* Oxford: Blackwell, 1992.
Mourelatos, Alexander, ed. *The Pre-Socratics: A Collection of Critical Essays.* Princeton: Princeton University Press, 1994.
Moyal, Georges J.D., ed. *René Descartes: Critical Assessments,* vol. II. London: Routledge, 1991.
Nehamas, Alexander. "Self-Predication And Plato's Theory Of Forms", reprinted in Terence Irwin (ed.), pp. 195-205.
Nietzsche, Friedrich. *Sämmtliche Werke: Kritische Studienausgabe in 15 Einzelbaenden,* Vol. 6. Berlin: De Gruyter, 1988.
Nozick, Robert. *Anarchy, State, And Utopia.* Malden: Basic Books, 1974.
Nussbaum, Martha. *The Fragility Of Goodness: Luck And Ethics In Greek Tragedy And Philosophy.* Cambridge: Cambridge University Press, 1986.
O'Connor, John, ed. *Modern Materialism: Readings On Mind-Body Identity.* New York: Harcourt, 1969.
Paul, Ellen Frankel et. al., eds. *Autonomy.* Cambridge: Cambridge University Press, 2003.
Penner, Terry. *The Ascent From Nominalism: Some Existence Arguments In Plato's Middle Dialogues.* Dordrecht: Reidel, 1987.
——. "Socrates And The Early Dialogues", in Richard Kraut (ed.), pp. 121-169.
——. "The Unity Of Virtue", reprinted in Gail Fine (ed.), vol 2, pp. 67-88.
Plato. *The Dialogues Of Plato,* Edith Hamilton and Huntington Cairns (eds.). Princeton: Princeton University Press, 1961.
——. The Dialogues Of Plato, transl. Benjamin Jowett, 3rd ed. Oxford: Clarendon, 1892.
Popkin, Richard H. et. al., eds. *The Columbia History of Western Philosophy.* New York: Columbia University Press, 1998.
Popper, Karl. *Die Logik der Forschung.* Vienna: Springer, 1935.
——. The Open Society And Its Enemies, Vol. 1. Princeton: Princeton University Press, 1962.
Press, Gerald A. "Plato", in Richard H. Popkin et. al. (eds.), pp. 32-52.
Prior, William. *Unity And Development In Plato's Metaphysics.* Chicago: Open Court, 1985.
Psillos, Stathis. *Causation And Explanation.* Montreal: McGill University Press, 2003.
Putnam, Hilary. *Mind, Language, And Reality.* Cambridge: Cambridge University Press, 1975.
Quine, Willard Van. *Word & Object.* Cambridge, Mass.: MIT Press, 1960.

Rapp, Christof, and Horn, Christoph. "Intuition und Methode: Abschied von einem Dogma der Platon- und Aristotelesexegese", in Uwe Meixner & Albert Newen (eds.), pp. 75-95.
Reeve, C.D.C. *Philosopher-Kings: The Argument Of Plato's Republic*. Princeton: Princeton University Press, 1988.
Rey, Georges. *Contemporary Philosophy Of Mind: A Contentiously Classical Approach.* Oxford: Blackwell, 1997.
Roochnik, David. "Socrates' Use of the *Techne*-Analogy," *The Journal of the History of Philosophy* 24 (1986), 295-310.
Robinson, Richard. *Plato's Earlier Dialectic*, 2nd edition. Oxford: Clarendon Press, 1953.
Rosenthal, David M., ed. *The Nature Of Mind*. Oxford: Oxford University Press, 1991.
Ross, W.D. *The Right And The Good*. Oxford: Oxford University Press, 1930.
Sartre, Jean-Paul. *Being And Nothingness: An Essay On Phenomenological Ontology*, transl. Hazel Barnes. London: Routledge, 2003.
Scarre, Geoffrey. *Utilitarianism*. London: Routledge, 1996.
Searle, John. *Expression And Meaning: Studies In The Theory Of Speech Acts*. Cambridge: Cambridge University Press, 1979.
——. *Intentionality*. Cambridge: Cambridge University Press, 1983.
Sen, Amartya et. al., eds. *Utilitarianism And Beyond*. Cambridge: Cambridge University Press, 1982.
Silverman, Allan. *The Dialectic Of Essence: A Study Of Plato's Metaphysics*. Princeton: Princeton University Press, 2002.
Singer, Peter, ed. *A Companion To Ethics*. Oxford: Blackwell, 1991.
Snell, Bruno. *The Discovery Of The Mind In Greek Philosophy And Literature*, transl. T.G. Rosenmeyer. New York: Dover, 1982.
Sosa, Ernest, ed. *Causation And Conditionals*. Oxford: Oxford University Press, 1974.
Stevenson, C. L. *Ethics And Language*. New Haven: Yale University Press, 1944.
Taylor, A.E. *Plato: The Man And His Work*, 4th ed. London: Dover, 1937.
Taylor, C.C.W. *Socrates*. Oxford: Oxford University Press, 1998.
Teloh, Henry. *Socratic Education In Plato's Early Dialogues*. Notre Dame: University Of Notre Dame Press, 1986.
Vendler, Zeno. *Res Cogitans:* An Essay in Rational Psychology. Ithaca, N.Y.: Cornell University Press, 1972.
Vico, Giambattista. *New Science*. London: Penguin, 1999.
Vlastos, Gregory. "Happiness And Virtue In Socrates' Moral Theory", reprinted in *Socrates: Ironist And Moral Philosopher*, pp. 200-232.
——, ed. *Plato: A Collection Of Critical Essays*, 2 Vols. Garden City, N.Y.: Doubleday, 1971.
——. *Platonic Studies*, 2nd ed. Princeton: Princeton University Press, 1981.
——. *Socrates: Ironist And Moral Philosopher*. Cambridge: Cambridge University Press, 1991.
Watson, Gary, ed. *Free Will*. Oxford: Oxford University Press, 1982.
Wedberg, A. "The Theory Of Forms", in: Gregory Vlastos (ed.), *Plato*, vol. 1, pp. 28-52.
Wierzbicka, Anna. *English Speech Act Verbs:* A Semantic Dictionary. Sydney: AcademicPress, 1987.
Wittgenstein, Ludwig. *Philosophische Untersuchungen*. Frankfurt: Suhrkamp, 2003.

www.ingramcontent.com/pod-product-compliance
Lightning Source LLC
Chambersburg PA
CBHW052051300426
44117CB00012B/2079